Visionary Poetics

Other Books by Robert D. Denham

Northrop Frye: An Enumerative Bibliography [1974]

Northrop Frye on Culture and Literature (ed.) [1978]

Northrop Frye and Critical Method [1978]

Northrop Frye: An Annotated Bibliography of Primary and Secondary Sources [1987]

Myth and Metaphor: Selected Essays by Northrop Frye, 1974-1987 (ed.) [1990]

Visionary Poetics

Essays on Northrop Frye's Criticism

Edited by Robert D. Denham
and Thomas Willard

PETER LANG
New York · San Francisco · Bern
Frankfurt am Main · Paris · London

Library of Congress Cataloging-in-Publication Data

Visionary poetics : essays on Northrop Frye's criticism /
edited by Robert D. Denham and Thomas Willard.
     p. cm.
     Includes bibliographical references and index.
     1. Frye, Northrop — Criticism and interpretation.
2. Frye, Northrop. Anatomy of criticism.   3. Criticism.
I. Willard, Thomas.
PN75.F7V57   1991   801'.95'092 — dc20   90-15518
ISBN 0-8204-1216-3   CIP
ISBN 0-8204-1217-1 (set of 3)

Cover drawing courtesy of Van Howell

The paper in this book meets the guidelines for permanence and
durability of the Committee on Production Guidelines for
Book Longevity of the Council on Library Resources.

3693

Contents

Preface

This book of essays had its beginnings in two programs devoted to Northrop Frye's work at the 1987 convention of the Modern Language Association in San Francisco. The year of Frye's seventy-fifth birthday seemed an appropriate time to recognize his achievement. We saw the occasion, however, not simply as a celebration, but as an opportunity for stepping back from the large body of Frye's work to consider its place in the world of contemporary critical thought. Accordingly, we asked three speakers—Hazard Adams, David Staines, and Imre Salusinszky—to consider the contexts of Frye's criticism. Three other speakers—Hayden White, Patricia Parker, and Paul Hernadi—were asked to reflect on *Anatomy of Criticism* thirty years after. Each of the papers that emerged focused on an issue decidedly central to the critical vision Frye has developed over his long career—a career now spanning almost six decades of published work.

In the first program, Hazard Adams considered the role that the anatomy as a literary genre has played in Frye's own work, and the ways that *Anatomy of Criticism*, because it both dissects literature into its constituent forms and then incorporates all forms into itself, becomes a work of art as well as a work of "science." David Staines examined a less well-known dimension of Frye's criticism—the more than eighty published essays and reviews of English-Canadian literature that taken together constitute an unparalleled contribution to Canadian literary culture. Imre Salusinszky examined Frye's revisionary view of nineteenth-century theories of the imagination, arguing that Frye's neo-Romanticism extended the powers of prophecy from the poet to the critic and so enabled him to circumvent the critical wars underway when he was writing the *Anatomy*.

In the second program, Hayden White argued against those who claim that *Anatomy of Criticism* is ideologically impure because it is ahistorical, and he maintained that Frye's modal understanding of history, which is similar to Kant's, is more able to represent history as a system undergoing constant changes in both its form and its contents than positivist and formalist views of history. Beginning with the different readings of Mallarmé by Frye and de Man, Patricia Parker examined the divergent directions taken by these two critics in the formalist tradition, concluding that Frye's view of metaphorical identity retains a temporal, dynamic, and revolutionary element that extends the vision of the function of metacriticism and the role of the critic in society. Finally, Paul Hernadi discussed Frye's views on the difference between literary and nonliterary language, arguing that Frye's ambiguous position (*ratio* both contains and is contained by *oratio*) distinguishes him from both the formalists, who sharply separate the literary and the nonliterary, and the poststructuralists, who do not.

The six original papers, necessarily brief in their original form, have been revised and expanded in the meantime for this collection. Northrop Frye's own talk, presented as the opening paper, gave a general overview of the questions that have been at the center of his critical life from the time of his early interest in Blake to his current work on the Bible. Frye's talk, which we reproduce as it was presented, rather uncannily foreshadows many of the broad issues raised by the other papers. Our own contributions represent considerable expansions of the remarks we made in introducing the two programs.

In *The Magic Mountain* Thomas Mann remarks that "seven is a good handy figure in its way, picturesque, with a savor of the mythical." Glancing at those anniversaries that punctuate Northrop Frye's career, we are reminded that Mann's "good handy figure" does have a mythical savor. The year of our gathering in San Francisco marked the fortieth and thirtieth anniversaries of *Fearful Symmetry* (1947) and *Anatomy of Criticism* (1957); Frye was first appointed as a lecturer in the honor course in English literature at Victoria College in 1937, the same year he was married; and in

1967, Canada's centenary year, he delivered the Whidden Lectures, later published as *The Modern Century*. If the number seven is mythical, in Frye's case it seems to be a particularly good example of the myth of the eternal return. In any case, we are pleased to offer to a wider public the papers of the seven participants, along with our own modest contributions, the *Schriftfest* in San Francisco having now become something like a *Festschrift*.

We record our gratitude here to Northrop Frye for participating in our program and to the six other contributors. We also express our thanks to Norman O. London, Academic Relations Officer of the Canadian Embassy, and to Lisa Svobda, Academic Relations Consul of the Canadian Consulate in New York City, for their generous support of our project; and to the English Programs office of the Modern Language Association for sponsoring the original convention programs.

Robert D. Denham
Thomas Willard

For Evelyn Denham

and

For Christopher and Gregory Willard

Auguries of Experience

Northrop Frye

In days so remote that I can barely remember them now, I was reading books on Blake in preparation for writing one myself. In those early times it was an unquestioned axiom that one should read everything available on a subject before trying to write about it, and for Blake in the thirties that was still humanly possible. So I immersed myself in the two or three good books and the hundred and fifty or so bad ones that had been devoted to Blake up to that time. One of the bad ones quoted a couplet from "Auguries of Innocence":

> He who the Ox to wrath has mov'd
> Shall never be by Woman lov'd

and objected that a poet less mentally confused would know that it was quite possible to be both brutal to animals and attractive to women. The critic forgot to look at the word "shall," and also forgot to take the title of the poem into account. I was still so green that it took me a while to work this out, but when I did I had a new insight into Blake and had acquired the first of my own auguries of experience, that is, the scaled-down expectations acquired from one's own life. Good books may instruct, but bad ones are more likely to inspire. Since then, as the author of criticism which some have found useful and others objectionable, I trust I have done something to inspire as well as instruct.

After finishing my Blake book, I went on to the *Anatomy of Criticism*, which in the innocent fifties, when it was published, was regarded, even by me, as an essay on critical theory. So in a way it was, although my conception of theory has always been different from those generally held. In this age of structural, poststructural, feminist, phenomenological, Marxist, metahistorical, dialogist, and any number of other schools, the word theory is essentially pluralistic: a theory is one of many dialectical formulations that proceed from specific assumptions and conclude with special emphases. My own conception of theory, though in many respects it may look much the same, is closer to the Greek *theoria*, a vision or conspectus of the area of literature, an area distinguishable from, though with a context relating it to, the other arts and the other forms of verbal discourse.

From this point of view there is a very broad consensus among all critical schools, a consensus which the variety of dialectical approaches more or less deliberately conceals. In the *Anatomy of Criticism* I pointed out the existence of this consensus, and even made suggestions for promoting it. Such suggestions look very naive now, and I have no longer any interest in making them. The procedure is rather like proposing the union of the various Christian churches on the ground that they accept most of the same major doctrines, or say they do. It is of course the differentiating dialectics and the special interests of conflicting groups that fill the foreground, and fill it so completely that the area of agreement remains largely unexamined, as no one is interested in it except the charitable.

This is my fortieth year as an MLA member, and so I have just acquired what is called, somewhat ironically, a life membership. Forty years ago literary criticism was dominated by a rather narrow historical approach to criticism which was neither genuinely historical nor genuinely critical. The first MLA meetings I attended resounded with the triumphs of this approach in the seminar rooms and with complaints about it in the corridors. A superstition grew up in graduate schools that only the obscurest aspects of the obscurest poets were still available for thesis material, and that the whole industry was approaching stagnation and exhaustion. When any discipline gets to this point, it blows up and a new conception of it takes its place, as happened in physics around 1900, when Planck and Einstein blew up its nineteenth-century mechanical synthesis. Similarly, it is now taken for granted that not only is the variety of individual works of literature inexhaustible, but the variety of critical treatments of them is equally so.

My own scholarly deficiencies in contemporary critical theory do not imply indifference, much less hostility, to what in itself is a most lively and exhilarating cultural growth. Even if it were not, its development was inevitable if we are to maintain the ideal that everyone on a university staff should be a productive scholar. Whether this ideal is either possible or desirable is not the point; it exists, and it cannot continue to exist without a large number of school badges, so to speak, ensuring one of a seat in front of a cue screen that will suggest some specific critical approach in advance. I have been assigned a badge of sorts myself, usually reading "mythical" or "archetypal," but my view of a latent consensus keeps me in a middle-of-the-road position, cherishing the belief of my age group that in all polarized situations there is much to be said on both sides. The only disadvantage of this position is that so much is *said* on both sides. My Canadian criticism, for example, has led to my being called a formalist critic who ignores or is unaware of the relation between literature and society, and to my being called a thematic critic who exaggerates that relation. I can only feel that as long as the two groups of objectors are approximately equal in numbers, I am still more or less on course, or at least on my course.

No one questions, or is ever likely to question, the right of literary scholars to discuss critical issues indefinitely. What could be questioned is whether the present critical activity exists for its own sake, a type of glass bead game, or whether it is going somewhere in the direction of increased and progressive understanding of both literature and criticism. Despite Enobarbus, nothing is staled by custom more quickly than infinite variety. This would be true even if all the infinite variety were new, but I keep finding also that venerable critical fallacies, whose funerals I thought I had attended many years ago, were not, as I had assumed, buried, but merely stuffed into cryonic refrigerators to await revival in future journals of theory.

Such issues may not matter in themselves, but a crisis may arise when the question of critical debate is confronted by the question of curriculum, of what should be taught to students, or at least undergraduates, over a limited period of time. There is always public concern over what the public is paying for, and the explosive success of some recent books that seem to be largely repeating what many teachers have been saying for half a century indicates one more revival of that concern. I have been listening to such expressions of concern most of my life, and have spent a fair proportion of my own critical energies on trying to do something about them. Another augury of experience I acquired in this process was that all such movements tend to focus on something we shall assuredly never get: a Messianic super-Archimedes who can say: "Give me a place to stand, and I will move the educational bureaucracy." But this time the dissatisfaction does seem to reflect back, however indirectly, on the critical situation I have been discussing. It is as though a psychiatric patient, already hundreds of dollars in arrears, had suddenly realized that his treatment was by definition interminable.

I happen to be one of those who believe that contemporary criticism is going somewhere, although my notion of where it is going antedates most of the activity itself, and has changed very little since. I have spoken of a vision of literature, because I think that there is a literary universe, which, like every other universe, is unbounded and finite. The variety of individual literary works may be infinite; the total body of what can be produced as literature is not. Any given period of criticism, no doubt every period, may have too narrow a view of this total body. The permanent value of, for example, women's studies or black studies is in reminding criticism of the narrowness of its scope of recognition. But there is a totality to what the mythical and imaginative forms of verbal discourse can do: they may be unlimited in depth and complexity, but they are finite in range.

It was this conviction that led me, in the *Anatomy of Criticism*, to consider what I called encyclopedic forms, works of a scope that seemed to suggest a circumference within which the verbal creative imagination operates. Such forms include some epics, some novels, and, above all, sacred books. They also include mythologies, cosmologies, like those incorporated into Dante and Milton, cosmological principles like the chain of being, and ideologies in their primary, or mythical, shape. Such frameworks are always imaginative, and hence literary, in origin, however much science or political theory may be called in to rationalize them. Of the sacred books, the central one for a Western critic was the Bible. The Bible is the only place in our tradition I know where one can get a view of literature that goes beyond literature, and so establishes its relative finiteness, and yet includes all the elements of literature. In this age of posts and metas, I can find nothing in our cultural tradition except the Bible that really illustrates the metaliterary.

It then occurred to me, after finishing the *Anatomy*: suppose one were to reverse the process, starting with the structure of the Bible, and working outwards to literature? No one would attempt a study of Islamic culture without starting with the Koran, or of Hindu culture without starting with the Vedas and Upanishads. I hesitated for many years before attempting to say anything about this, but another augury of experience, this time directly derived from Blake, pushed me toward writing: the axiom not to trust prudence, and to persist in folly. The preliminary study that I produced in 1982, *The Great Code*, bore the subtitle: "The Bible and Literature." The operative word was "and": all studies of the Bible as literature that I had read treated the literary aspect of the Bible as incidental, even as ornamental.

It seemed obvious to me that while the Bible can hardly be called a work of literature, every word of it is written in the literary language of myth and metaphor. By myth I mean story or narrative (*mythos*), and by metaphor a verbal formula of identity. These are the central elements of literature, but in literature itself they are hypothetical: in the Bible they are existential, incorporating the reader with a completeness that literature cannot attempt. So in the Bible a literary texture forms the content of something else. For this something else I retained the term *kerygma*, proclamation or revelation, even though that meant opposing the formidable authority of Rudolf Bultmann, for whom kerygma and myth are mutually exclusive. I am now engaged in disentangling myself from the final chapter of a sequel to this book.

I can hardly hope to summarize a complex argument in the minute or two I have left, but a few suggestions about it may interest you. Literature seems to me to revolve around what I call the primary concerns of humanity, those that have to do with freedom, love, and staying alive, along with the ironies of their frustration, as distinct from the secondary or ideological concerns of politics and religion, for which the direct verbal expression is expository rather than literary. Because the content of literature is hypothetical, assumed rather than asserted, it has always been regarded as a form of verbal play, and it is only recently that we have come to understand that play may well be more important than the serious activities promoted by ideology, such as going to war or exploiting other people or the other lives in nature. As long as the kerygma or proclamation of the Bible is opposed to myth, it will be identical with ordinary ideological rhetoric; when it is made to include myth, it gives us a new perspective on the social function of literature. By squeezing a mythical and metaphorical proclamation into one book, however long and inexhaustible a book, the Bible provides a kind of experimental model for what I have called the finiteness of literature. Once again, what I mean by finiteness is not something that limits or imposes barriers, but something that allows for a progressive increase of understanding.

Naturally the Bible, being a historical product even though it transcends history, cannot avoid suggesting specific Jewish and Christian ideologies, and one has to try to set out its mythical and metaphorical structure as something distinct from them. It should go without saying that this applies even more obviously to all the authoritarian, patriarchal, sexist, racist, and sectarian ideologies that profess to derive from the Bible, as well as from doctrinal and other aspects of what is usually meant by "religion," which is still an ideology expressed in rhetorical or hortatory language.

I was asked recently why I could never write anything without mentioning Shakespeare's *Tempest*. The reason is that I know of no other work of literature that illustrates more clearly the inter-change of illusion and reality which is what literature is all about. In drama the illusion on the stage is the reality, and *The Tempest* is a play about the creation of a play through Prospero's magic, where illusion becomes the raw material for a new creation, while the old objective reality turns into illusion in its turn and disappears, leaving not a rack behind. The Bible similarly begins with the creation, the presenting of objective order to a conscious mind, and ends with a new creation. It is written throughout in the language of myth and metaphor because that is the language of illusion. Freud was quite right, however unconsciously, in talking about "the future of an illusion," because nothing can possibly have a future except an illusion. "Reality" can only be what does not change or changes entirely on its own terms: as far as we are concerned, its future has already occurred. But when we wake up from a dream in our bedroom, we are confronted, not with "reality," but with a collection of human artifacts. The essential "reality principle," then, consists of what human beings have made, and what human beings have made they can remake. Whether they will or not will depend on the strength of the illusory desires expressed in their dreams.

All this can be taught by literature alone, but literature alone gives us only a relative perspective; every way of turning illusion into reality is equally valid within its orbit. One needs also to try to get outside literature without simply returning to ideology. I am certainly no Moses proposing to lead criticism out of Egypt and a plague of darkness, though I may resemble Moses in not having any very clear notion where the Promised Land really is. On the contrary—and this is my last augury of experience—for many years now I have been addressing myself primarily, not to other critics, but to students and a nonspecialist public, realizing that whatever new directions can come to my discipline will come from their needs and their intense if unfocused vision.

I. Northrop Frye and the Contexts of Criticism

The Visionary Education

Thomas Willard

> *"Every breakthrough in education*
> *is a breakthrough in vision."*
> —Northrop Frye on Education

Some years ago, Northrop Frye had the opportunity to speak about his former teacher and colleague E. J. Pratt. He revered Pratt as the epic poet of Canada, and had edited Pratt's poems "as an act of personal homage to the poet in his seventy-fifth year" ("Editor's Preface" xii). He remembered Pratt fondly as a person, and liked to tell stories of Pratt's legendary absent-mindedness—the day, for example, when Pratt stopped his car at a traffic light, got out to help an elderly woman onto the streetcar, and took the streetcar to Victoria College while his own car was still running. But he realized that only Pratt's cultural position, as a highly civilized man in an emerging nation, could in any way account for the poetry itself. He therefore decided to set Pratt in context, specifically "in the context of modern poetry, and in the further context of the relation of modern poetry to modern civilization" (*Bush Garden* 181), knowing that for Pratt civilization revolved about the University of Toronto. I feel a similar compulsion in writing about my former teacher and supervisor in the year of his seventy-fifth birthday (1987).[1] I want to locate Frye's efforts, very broadly, in the context of modern criticism, and this by way of introduction to the other essays in this section. But I also want to say something about the social context of his criticism, which for Frye starts in the vocational context of the undergraduate classroom. Teaching has been a vocation for him, as he explained when he spoke on Pratt: his three English professors of sixty years ago held up an ideal that he found irresistible. He has repeatedly said that all his books are "teachers' manuals" or "teaching books" (*Great Code* xiv; *Divisions* 181), and I think they will make better sense to those who know something of his educational views.

"Context" is an important word for Frye because it provides a link between the literary text and everything else. In *The Critical Path: An Essay on the Social Context of Literary Criticism*, where the word resounds with the regularity of a quarter-hour chime, Frye remarks that his critical theory began with two questions: Where does criticism belong? and How does poetry produce meaning? (14-15).[2] The first question led him to talk about mythology as the total expression of a society's concern, and the second led him to distinguish two types of context: the everyday world of objects, to which ordinary discourse belongs, and a self-contained world of imagination with all its poetic embodiments. In the terms of an older age, these are Sidney's brazen and golden worlds, but they are inseparable for Frye because the everyday world is built on myths like Back to Basics and Star Wars, while the imaginative world is the truly mythological. Criticism cannot develop a sense of its larger function as a key to such diverse mythologies as those in Thomism, Marxism, and Darwinism unless it has formed a sense of its narrower function as a study of myths and their literary expression.

To the first question—Where does criticism belong?—Frye responds that it must not be considered a subgenre of literature, like the travelogue, but an autonomous subject outside literature. To the second—How does poetry produce meaning?—he says it does not refer primarily to the physical world, as a dictionary does, but to other poetry and to the imaginative world. He thinks of criticism as an applied social science, based on the inductive study of literature and the humanities, and he thinks of literature as a self-supporting structure, the "total order of words" of which T. S. Eliot wrote. In the "Polemical Introduction" to *Anatomy of Criticism*, where he gives these thoughts their fullest, most memorable expression, he challenges critics who deny the autonomy of their enterprise and so regard criticism as a "parasite." Of these critics, some look for meaning outside literature, most often in a religious or philosophical or political and historical framework; while others, who are "critics" mainly in the way that the entertainment media use the word, have quite personal agendas for holding their thumbs up or down. The first group gives us various sorts of "determinism"—Freudian, Marxist, and so forth—while the other produces "value judgments," sending the critical stock of authors on new (and largely arbitrary) cycles of boom and bust. No other remarks of Frye's have caused so much controversy as these.

If critics are to avoid determinisms and value judgments, says Frye, they must first consider a literary work in context, which means in the author's total *oeuvre* or canon and in the whole of literature. They may then ask what the work says about the society that produced it or what it can say to an intelligent reader in our society. If we apply these principles to Frye's work, and read his books as he reads Blake's, we must first ask where a book belongs in his critical output. With *The Critical Path*, for example, we have a return to principles that he first articulated in *Anatomy of Criticism* and a response to the crisis on North American campuses during the days of "student unrest." With the *Anatomy*, we have the central work of his productive career—an outgrowth of his early book on Blake and an anticipation of his recent work on the Bible and literature. To borrow Erik Erikson's notion of the major life crises, which Frye has borrowed to other ends, we may regard *Fearful Symmetry* as the book that established his critical identity, *Anatomy of Criticism* as the one that brought his critical theory to full maturity, and *The Great Code* and *Words with Power* as efforts to integrate lifelong concerns of his criticism and teaching. This may seem a more pertinent analogy for a creative writer, but Frye is well aware that criticism can be an art. In the essay that follows this one, Frye's longtime follower Hazard Adams addresses the paradox of a critical science that becomes the art it anatomizes. In doing so, Adams is thrown back into the mythic material from which Frye began his study of Blake.

For the true writer is a "liar," as Oscar Wilde remarked in "The Decay of Lying"—an essay which, Frye says, "modern theories of criticism have been annotating in more garbled language ever since" (*Creation* 5). Sidney's term for this lying is "fabling"; Frye's is some variant of "myth-making." In *The Critical Path*, he responds to the charge that he has rewritten his own personal myth in every book, saying that he "would never read or trust any writer who did not also do so" (9). Although he has never identified a myth as peculiarly his, it might well be the myth of hooking the leviathan. This begins as a last bullying challenge that God lays on Job: "Canst thou draw out leviathan with an hook?" (41:1). It produces the Jewish tradition, which Jessie Weston records in *From Ritual to Romance* (128), that the Messiah will hook the leviathan in the last days—a tradition based on the statement in Psalm 74:14 that God fed the wandering Israelites with the slain leviathan. In Blake, the leviathan becomes the symbolic equivalent of the physical sea of time and space. In Frye, it becomes the whole of experience as viewed from outside; we have to escape the leviathan, Jonah-like, before we can see the divine scheme, and until we escape we are prisoners of a sort. (Hence the *New Yorker* cartoon with the caption: "Jonah! When did you get out?") Frye treats the myth repeatedly: in *Fearful Symmetry* on the tyranny of nature and society (139-43), in the *Anatomy* on myth and romance (189-92), in *The Great Code* on the victory over the body of death (187-92). He has used the monster myth to conclude his fall semester of lectures on the Bible; and in closing his response to the English Institute session on his work, he painted the monster that the humanist faces in the classroom, the hydra-headed representation of the social mythology, and conceded, "No one person, certainly no one critic, can kill this dragon who guards our word-hoard" ("Reflections" 146). The dragon-slaying myth brings out the best in Frye, so it seems strangely appropriate that the main campus of the University of Toronto, where he has spent his adult life, is commonly known after one main thoroughfare as the St. George Campus.

If we proceed with contexts, we must now place Frye's work in society, which is to say in Canada and at Victoria College, where he earned degrees in arts and divinity and progressed through the teaching ranks to become department chair, principal, and chancellor. Frye received his graduate education at Merton College, Oxford, where he kept the minutes of the literary society.[3] His approach to graduate instruction, at least, has been more British than American in emphasizing independent research rather than seminars. However, he belongs to the postwar generation of Canadians who found the cultural dominance of Britain yielding to that of the United States. Like many of Canada's creative writers, he has found his main audience in the U.S. and has written in a North American rather than a British idiom. He tends to revel in American slang, especially in classroom lectures like those transcribed for *Northrop Frye on Shakespeare*. Nevertheless, he has neither been swallowed by the leviathan below the forty-ninth parallel nor become a nationalist of the sort that surfaced during the Vietnam era, the parody Yankee who covers his nakedness with a maple leaf. Having learned from Blake that home is wherever you hang your hat, he has celebrated Canada as the first country to grow up in the spirit of internationalism. He has done a good deal to help younger Canadians take their world and their art seriously. His view that place is the real question facing Canadians — a view summed up in his memorable riddle "Where is here?" — has influenced a generation of writers. To cite only one example, Margaret Atwood used the title *Where Is Here?* for the early drafts of her novel *Surfacing*, and drew so directly from Frye in her "Thematic Guide to Canadian Literature" that a reissue was attacked, by Paul Stuewe, in an issue of *Books in Canada*, that asked on the cover: "What's Wrong with Northrop Frye?"[4] In the third essay of this section, David Staines provides further (and more accurate) information on Frye's work as a critic of Canadian literature. The Canadian context deserves to be much better known, if only because it shows Frye in the practical work of a poetry reviewer who must make judgments of a sort.

From Frye's physical surroundings, we may proceed to the tradition where he has felt his strongest affinities: the left-wing strain in English literature as it runs from Spenser and Milton through Blake and Yeats, a visionary mythmaking Protestantism where the

Biblical Word has found increasingly personal manifestations. Frye's book on Blake made a major contribution to the study of English Romanticism, but it was also what he would call a recreation of Romanticism. The book began by rearticulating Blake's "argument" or, as Frye said in the preface to the Beacon paperback edition, "recreating Blake's thought and attitude in my own words" (v). In the process, Frye had to rethink such basic questions as the working of the imagination. He concluded that when Blake described the rising sun as a Sanctus chorus, he was not "imagining things" or groping to describe the once-in-a-lifetime experience of a Juliana or Pascal: Blake was recreating the sunrise in poetic language, much as Hazlitt would recreate a boxing match in prose. Similarly, Frye was not just paraphrasing Blake but recreating his system, so that Blake provided him mainly with a system of reading literature. This recreation was so much Frye's own that readers have found it requires (and rewards) a different order of reading than most literary criticism — even the wag who complained that, by the time he finally understood Frye, he had long since understood Blake. Imre Salusinszky writes of this recreation as an "extension" of Romanticism and, in the final essay of this section, places Frye's extended or neo-Romanticism in a literary movement that includes Wallace Stevens and Harold Bloom.

It would be futile to seek a "master context" for Frye — whether in art or in Canadian letters or in the study of Romanticism or Shakespeare or the Bible. Any context one might offer to put all the others into their proper place would quickly become a determinism, and would have to face the competing claims of all other possible contexts. Nevertheless, it seems useful to consider the claims of one context, especially in a critic who has been consistent to the point of the occasional repetition. In the remaining paragraphs, I want to consider Frye in the context of education. I shall not try to expound his theories of educating the imagination — he does this quite well himself — but I want to provide some background for these theories and then to suggest some implications they have for readers of his work.

In the days when Marshall McLuhan's reputation was at its peak—when the *Laugh-In* television program regularly asked what he had been doin' and when *Time* quoted Frye as a "disciple"—Tom Wolfe wrote that it was impossible to understand McLuhan without learning about such esoterica as carrels and common rooms (31).[5] The same could be said of Frye, only we would have to add abstractions like the honor course. When they entered the University of Toronto in 1928, arts students could elect a three- or a four-year degree program. Students taking a four-year degree were almost invariably enrolled in an honors program; indeed, Frye contributed an editorial to the college paper calling for an end to the pass course. Frye enrolled in the honor course in Philosophy and English, devised by the philosopher G. S. Brett, who became the first editor of the *University of Toronto Quarterly* when Frye was still an undergraduate (*Divisions* 27). The student's curriculum was closely prescribed in the annual calendar, with set courses and authors for each year, so that the student would progress through four hundred years of English literature and European thought in the course of four years. Frye finished first in the class each year, and while he wrote an editorial at the time to complain that the exam system adversely affected one's view of literature,[6] he later remarked that preparing simultaneously for examinations in Milton and Descartes gave one the feeling that one had the seventeenth century down cold. The honor degree was offered until 1969, when it was "swept away in a great wave of exuberant hysteria" (*Divisions* 152). Frye's uncharacteristically bitter tone indicates just how strongly he felt: Toronto had thrown away a program that many universities would have paid dearly to get.

A related term, for Frye, is the federated college. The University of Toronto is made up of separate colleges, and the liberal arts colleges were originally divided along religious lines. Victoria, where Frye studied and taught, is affiliated with the United Church of Canada (uniting the Methodist and Congregational movements); St. Michael's, where McLuhan taught, is Roman Catholic; Trinity is Anglican; and University is nondenominational, as are the newer "constituent" colleges: Erindale, Innis, New, and Scarborough. Until 1975, there were many English departments within the university, including a graduate department that drew from all the undergraduate ones. For students, this meant smaller classes and a better chance to meet the professors in one's college and begin to feel part of a college community. For professors, it meant a greater opportunity to teach the full range of literature classes. Frye has remarked how fortunate he felt to be able to teach Milton beside two great Miltonists: A. S. P. Woodhouse at UC, and Arthur Barker at Trinity (*Spiritus* 12). In response to the frequent charge that he has imposed an a priori frame on literature, he likes to recall his first year of full-time teaching, in 1939, when he taught four honor courses, covering four hundred years of literature. "I could not *move* outside the texts I was teaching," he told one interviewer. "My concepts and categories took their shape from my reading" (Freedman). "He even associates his success with staying in Canada," says his biographer, John Ayre. "He thinks the compulsive competitiveness and specialization in the American universities would have destroyed the possibility of working on a broad range of literature" ("Mythological" 23). He grants that the old system was "intolerably inflexible and cumbersome" by the time that the baby boomers arrived, with too few opportunities for students and too many responsibilities for their teachers, but even now he points to the honor course and federated system as "the two things that put Toronto's English department among the best on the continent (at least)" ("Foreword" xii).

Like anyone else in higher education, Frye was drawn into the curricular debates of the 1960s. He heard the calls for greater coverage and (he hated the word) relevance. Although he was himself a powerful argument for the standard reading list or (to use his own term in a broader sense) the secular scripture, he found that he had provided ammunition for the assault on the old literary curriculum. As universities grew and departments with them, newer teachers sought their niche in courses organized by genre and symbol rather than historical period.[7] Such courses had hardly existed outside the advanced graduate seminar when the *Anatomy* went to press, with its essays on symbol and genre, but soon the number of "period" course requirements were reduced or replaced altogether. In turn, the new courses prepared the way for the "new literary history," which, with its emphasis on power, gender, and the rest, brought back the sort of determinisms that Frye had hoped to vanquish. Meanwhile, courses in minor figures proliferated. Frye again provided a powerful argument, this time against using hasty value judgments to dismiss an author as unworthy of serious attention. As a divinity student, he had learned the principle behind the minister's choice of a "text" for the next sermon: any verse in the Bible can become the center if properly considered. He would call this the "centripetal" drive, where the onward momentum of the plot yields to the inward penetration of the reading, and he might recall that writers like Joyce in *Finnegans Wake* have written as though every word were potentially *the* Word or Logos. He allowed that the study of a minor figure could lead to major finds, provided that the student did not lose sight of larger literary patterns.

In truth, Frye has mixed feelings about the teaching of contemporary or Canadian literature. Ideally, he would like professors to discuss their contemporaries as his teachers at Victoria College introduced him to Hemingway and Joyce, and as he has introduced students to Pynchon: by way of digression. His daunting references to recent works have the function of helping students to find their culture, to distinguish the good from the tawdry, and to become intelligent consumers of the arts. However, he realizes that there is a vast difference, psychologically, between having a leisure-time interest, say, in film and studying it in a formal course (Frye, "Foreword" xi). While he distrusts experimental courses of the sort that begin with Kerouac as "background" and move on to popular paperbacks, he sees even this as part of a natural process that will lead back to the classics (Oliver 34-35).

If there is an irony in the way that Frye's theories have been used to overthrow the honor course he so loved, there is a further irony in the current cries for "opening the canon" or "canonizing" authors who represent minority groups. When the *OED* was completed in Frye's youth, the only literary meaning of "canon" was the

Christian Bible and, by extension, the sacred scriptures of other religions.[8] When Frye studied divinity at Emmanuel College, in Victoria University, he learned that the word comes from the Greek word for "rule" in the sense of straightrule: it appears, for example, in Saint Paul's injunction "let us walk by the same rule, let us mind the same thing" (Philippians 3:16; see *Great Code* 200). When he wrote *Fearful Symmetry* and wanted to draw attention to Blake's "Prophetic Books," he reminded his reader that Blake took the trouble to engrave most of them, and that Blake thought of them, quite seriously, as a new or "Everlasting Gospel." Thus he said, "The engraved poems were intended to form an exclusive and definitive canon," conscious that he was stretching the use of this last word, and later: "Once we begin to look at Blake's engraved works as a canon, we can discern certain structural principles within it" (6, 187). As he used it, the word "canon" referred to a decision by the author rather than the critic, a feature to be discovered in the author's work rather than imposed on it. In one chapter, Frye juxtaposed "tradition" and "experiment," no doubt with an eye to Eliot's famous essay on "Tradition and the Individual Talent." Here he identified Blake's tradition, discussing authors whose works Blake studied and illustrated but also authors like William Langland and Thomas Vaughan, of whom he had probably never heard – authors, in any case, who followed the "Great Code" of art as Blake understood it from his reading of the Bible. Frye was well aware that Blake's tradition (and his own), being Romantic, Protestant, and revolutionary, was in every respect different from Eliot's.

Fearful Symmetry soon fell into the hands of Harold Bloom, then a freshman at Cornell, who has told Imre Salusinszky that he read it a hundred times and committed it to memory (*Criticism in Society* 18). A correspondence ensued, and a struggle between the critical father and son which culminated in Bloom's *Map of Misreading* (30) or perhaps in Bloom's essay on the killing of the father, which appeared in the "Fryeschrift" prepared to mark Frye's seventieth birthday. One major debt and difference involved the word "canon," which Bloom for all purposes conflated with "tradition."

When Frye's ecumenical approach to literature collided with Bloom's competitive view of poets, Bloom chose, in the words of David Fite, to "valorize" the visionary imagination and thus "erect—or resurrect—a much more circumscribed canon" (17). Bloom would not accept the notion of an "ideal order" in literature, which Frye had derived from Eliot, and Fite, at least, does not seem to recognize the differences between Eliot and Frye in matters of social or literary order (82). And so what had been a term of inclusion for Frye became one of exclusion.[9] Bloom would admit or exclude poets from his canon on the basis of certain criteria—he took years before admitting Robert Penn Warren to the canon of American poetry.

When the honor course was scuttled at Toronto, and the standard sequence of study was replaced by broad area requirements, Frye continued to hope for a planned program of secondary education. He had become interested in public education at an early stage because, as he told Ronald Bates, "I really didn't believe in my own theories until I found a way in which they could be taught to young students" (Bates 33). During the 1960s, he became involved with a grassroots curricular movement in Toronto, in which the schools and the university together designed the sort of coordinated program for primary and secondary students that was then available at the university. This group, in turn, was part of a large-scale effort in English education during the fifties and sixties, with some two dozen counterparts in the U.S. The educational historian Arthur N. Applebee notes that two figures dominated the attempts to reform English curricula: Jerome Bruner of Harvard, who provided such broad concepts as the open-ended or "spiral" curriculum, and Northrop Frye, who provided "the conceptualization of English needed to fit it into Bruner's mold: a series of basic structuring principles that could be discussed at increasingly complex levels" (202-3). Writing a decade after the effort ended without success, Applebee adds that few people appreciated Frye's insistence that a new curriculum would require a more comprehensive understanding of literary criticism than any one of the current critical schools offered, and that no one heeded Frye's call for using different sorts of criticism at different levels of education, with linguistic criticism in the elementary schools, myth criticism in the middle schools, and New Criticism in the high schools.

Frye edited the report of the Joint Committee of the Toronto Board of Education and the University of Toronto and wrote the introduction.[10] To his dismay, the provincial government moved in and created what he has since called an "educational Pentagon," staffed largely, it seemed, by Americans (*Divisions* 155). However, the curricular studies led indirectly to a series of twelve textbooks under the title *Literature: Uses of the Imagination*, for which Frye was the supervisory editor. Organized by theme and genre, the series was designed to help secondary school students discover repeating patterns in plot or image from both classic and contemporary works of literature. "This approach simplifies the study of literature," said the publisher's brochure, "because it gives it structure. Once students realize that literature is built on certain basic archetypal patterns, they will have acquired a structure which they can bring to all the literature they will ever read" (Harcourt 3). Outlining his plan for teaching literature systematically, Frye emphasized context and structure. The teacher should "establish a context within literature for each work being studied," and should teach "the structure of literature, and the content by means of the structure, so that the content can be seen to have some reason in the structure for existing" (*On Education* 111). And if we are to teach structure, it seemed to him, "We have no choice about teaching mythology": for our very lives are based on myths, and it is vitally important that we learn to recognize a pastoral myth when we see it, especially when we see it in politics (*On Education* 118, 124).[11]

Frye's educational theories are an extension and application of his critical theories, and he has been most successful where he has been most controversial. He has insisted on teaching structure, be it in myth and narrative, in symbol and imagery, in genre and convention, or in other constructs like national literatures and cultural periods. Indeed, he has pointed out that one cannot "teach" literature, strictly speaking, any more than one can teach nature or behavior: one can only teach facts about literature or chemicals, say, or economic activity, and Frye would like to regard the structure of taught facts about literature as criticism. By the same token, one cannot teach students how to read a poem satisfactorily, since reading is a private experience and a truly satisfactory experience may happen only rarely; one can only prepare students for such an experience by equipping them with a body of critical knowledge. Frye has met with surprising resistance to his premise about teaching criticism, which seemed to contain more common sense than revelation. Even Augustine had said as much, without intending a revolution in pedagogy, when he observed that "literature . . . could not be a discipline if there were no definitions in it, no distinctions and distributions into classes and parts" (*Soliloquies* xi, 20). But the success of Frye's teaching methods has offset the controversy as to whether his structures are useful heuristic and mnemonic devices or unnecessary abstractions. What counts, for him, is the confirmation that he has received from colleagues who say (with Geoffrey Hartman at the English Institute session devoted to his critical theory): "it works; it is teachable" ("Reflections" 137).

With his interest in the structural properties of literature, which long predated the popularity of European structuralism in English studies and indeed made him want to subtitle the *Anatomy* "Structural Poetics" (Levin 26), Frye has always talked of education in terms of seeing a subject rather than of imbibing knowledge (or being spoon-fed). "From kindergarten onwards," he has said, "the teacher is not instilling literature into a mind that doesn't know any, but reshaping the student's total verbal experience" (*Spiritus* 21). When he wrote his first published essay on education, in 1945, he argued that great literature offered a "vision of reality" from which political liberalism arises ("Liberal Education" 135). When he lectured at the Graduate School of Education at Harvard, he observed, "The good teacher is distinguished from his mediocre colleagues mainly by the efforts he makes to transform content into structure, to help his students to see significant patterns in facts" ("Developing Imagination" 35). When his textbook series was in preparation for secondary schools, he wrote in the accompanying essay that a person who teaches literature "is also trying to teach the ability to be aware of one's imaginative social vision, and so to escape the prison of unconscious social under- standing" (*On Education* 136). This preference derives, like much else, from Frye's study of Blake, and it has a direct counterpart in his critical theory and his emphasis on the visual element in the etymological root of "theory." Indeed, when he was asked recently whether his background in Romantic criticism has affected his teaching, Frye said:

> Teaching is a very difficult art. One of the first things to remember is that you are not the source of the student's knowledge. That is, teaching is not a matter of conveying information from somebody who has got it to somebody who has not. The teacher has to try to transform himself into a kind of trans- parent medium for whatever he is teaching. If he's lucky, there may come a point at which the entire classroom is pervaded by the spirit of the sub- ject—of Blake, or Shakespeare, or romance. And then the relationship between teacher and student, which in itself is a somewhat embarrassing rela- tionship, disappears, and you are all united in the same vision. ("Questions" 32)

Visionary education has several natural consequences for Frye's teaching style.

First, Frye makes extensive use of blackboard designs to illus- trate patterns in literature; the tables and figures in Part Two of *The Great Code* are representative, and first saw the light in his undergraduate course in the Mythological Framework of Western Culture. In the graduate seminar in the Principles of Literary Symbolism, which he taught for many years, he told students that he should simply give them a tarot pack of designs to shuffle on their own. Such illustrations have a mnemonic value for the stu- dent, and even for Frye, who says he trained himself to lecture with few if any notes. Second, he puts little emphasis on the sound of his voice. When reading aloud, he eschews "interpretation" of the sort associated with oral performance. Despite his lifelong fascina- tion with "the music of poetry," he tends to fall into a deep rhyth- mic monotone, with somewhat rounder vowels than his customary Down East deadpan, and he has said there are passages like the last lines of *Paradise Lost* that he will not read in public. Anyone who wonders how such a shy, unassuming person can draw such large audiences may find an answer in his visual metaphor: the teacher becomes transparent so that the author or subject can take over.

Frye's sense of the teacher's authority is ambivalent in a quite Socratic fashion. Socrates was the most unprepossessing of men, who claimed to know nothing but made it painfully obvious that most people knew still less. If a modern Socrates wandered into an MLA convention, he would probably say, "I'm a poor English teacher, and I couldn't afford to buy M. X's new book or attend Herr's Y institute, but if you'll be good enough to tell me what you learned I'll be glad to talk about it and try to understand his theory." This line of discussion tends to affirm the student's basic good sense, however, and to conceal the teacher's special learning. In the *Meno*, Socrates demonstrates that a young slave knows all the principles of geometry and needs only to remember them. As Frye puts it, the Socratic teacher "attempts to re-create the subject in the student's mind, and his strategy in doing this is first of all to get the student to recognize what he already potentially knows, which includes breaking up the powers of repression in his mind that keep him from knowing what he knows. That is why it is the teacher, rather than the student, who asks most of the questions" (*Great Code* xv). Frye's questions can be terrifying, at least when he waits one or two minutes for an answer, surveying the class with the penetrating gaze of a minister on stewardship Sunday. But he is tolerant of wrong answers, and even of wrongheaded questions. When a very confused young man once raised his hand and asked about his difficulty choosing between a blonde and brunette, Frye deftly turned the discussion to conventions of literary romance. When a feminist spent the better part of a semester holding him personally responsible for Milton's views on women, he responded sincerely and with interest, realizing that his own readers would have similar questions.[12]

Margaret Atwood, a student of thirty years ago, has observed Frye's classroom magic through a novelist's eye:

In Honours English, life was chronological and Milton came in the third year. Northrop Frye taught Milton. "Taught" isn't exactly the word. Frye said, "Let there be Milton," and lo, there was. It was done like this. He stood at the front of the room. He took one step forward, put his left hand on the table, took another step forward, put his right hand on the table, took a step back, removed his left hand, another step back, removed his right hand, and repeated the pattern. While he was doing this, pure prose, in real sentences and paragraphs, issued from his mouth. He didn't say "um," as most of us did, or leave sentences unfinished, or correct himself. I had never heard anyone do this before. It was like seeing a magician producing birds from a hat. You kept wanting to go around behind Frye or look under the table to see how he did it. (398-99)

Frye's phenomenal memory was partly responsible for this; he could open *The Student's Milton* to exactly the right page, and rumor had it that the three books on his desk in the principal's office at Vic (the Bible, Milton, and Blake) were there for decoration only as he knew them all by heart. Those long pauses also played a part, no doubt, as he tends to speak in paragraphs of perhaps five minutes each. But there was the irrefutable magic of seeing something born before one's eyes. The poet James Reaney has recalled his excitement in hearing Frye work out details of the *Anatomy* in a graduate course (28). Atwood, meanwhile, was listening to an early draft of *The Return of Eden*.[13]

Some students (and readers) inevitably conclude that Frye knows more than he lets on, and holds secrets into which they may one day be initiated in private. Frye has steadfastly refused to be anyone's guru, however, joking that one disciple in twelve will betray the master, as Judas did, and the other eleven will be like Peter, who denied Jesus three times. Following Blake, he tends to think that any sort of emanation or clone would be an abomination, true neither to himself nor the student, and he is glad if he can help the student to find an amenable "mentor" on the library shelves.[14] In conferences, he becomes rather like a Zen master, letting the visitor speak his or her mind without interruption and generally answer his or her question in the process. Even a short conference can thus seem very long. Of course, the reserve is a mark of his legendary shyness, but, while the shyness may be less of a convenient stereotype than Pratt's forgetfulness, it has helped him to survive as a writer amid the demands of university life. Occasionally, he must remind the visitor that he is at work on a major speech — in earlier decades it might have been a major university or government report — but he prefers a less imposing persona.

Frye sometime says modestly that Blake taught him everything he knows. Of course, he has had to make some accommodation for the poet who attributed the fixed text or code to Urizen, the "primeval Priest" and father of all error.[15] But Blake also taught him that the eternal world has room for all possible contrarieties, and this accords with Frye's personal preference for inclusiveness in education and for the ecumenical sort of criticism to which he refers in his "Auguries of Experience." From time to time he has been cast in the role of Urizen — most astonishingly, perhaps, in a series of diatribes against the "high priest of clerical obscurantism" that was issued in the sixties by a Maoist collective in Montreal (Kogan).[16] It may even be appropriate that the critic who has given us the "Orc cycle," as an enduring contribution to Blake studies, should have lived out the myth in his own life, becoming the purveyor of proverbial caution as well as prophetic enthusiasm.[17] I do not mean that he has become an apologist for a fixed tradition, where everything is in its place — this seems a complete misunderstanding of his position, however often it is repeated — nor that he has forged everything anew in his imagination, without reference to the social context of a work in the author's time or the reader's. Tradition and experiment converge for him, as much as for Blake; only he finds that it converges in education.

When Frye says his books are all "teaching books," he is speaking, first of all, as a tactful administrator. He has criticized commissions that would like to see the teacher's preparation time as being not much more than the student's,[18] and he once replied to a questionnaire by saying that he spent ten hours of preparation for every hour in the classroom. (This meant, in effect, that he was constantly preparing for classes.) The teaching/research dichotomy in modern academia seems a false dichotomy to Frye, who offers this aphorism: "A teacher who is not a scholar is soon going to be out of touch with his own subject, and a scholar who is not a teacher is soon going to be out of touch with the world" (*Divisions* 150). He has resisted the temptation of "research" professorships in the U.S., and when he retired from graduate teaching, as he entered semiretirement, he kept his undergraduate class in the Bible as a necessary part of his writing process. His remark about "teachers' manuals" gives us a key to his writing.

With the remark, Frye recalls a distinction between teaching and research that goes back at least to Bacon's *Advancement of Learning*: a distinction, in Bacon's terms, between "tradition" and "invention," the handing down of information and tools, such as Aristotelian logic, and the discovery of new tools and information. Bacon specified a different style for each type of discourse. Pedagogical speech or writing would be expository, but professional communication would be persuasive, as the scientist or philosopher, unlike the teacher, had to convince peers that a proposition or discovery was valid. Most academics will probably recognize a similar distinction in their own discourse, despite the considerable changes in the teacher's role since Bacon's day or even since Frye's youth — for example, the course evaluations which Frye has called a parody of the educational process (*Divisions* 152). We must persuade readers for presses and refereed journals far more than we must persuade even graduate students.

Frye's most persuasive book, in this respect, is *Fearful Symmetry*, which he wrote while in search of a publisher and which reflected only incidentally the wide ranging concerns of his undergraduate teaching experience. His most expository book, among his literary criticism, is probably *Northrop Frye on Shakespeare*, an edited transcript of his undergraduate lectures, and next to that *The Great Code*, the second half of which emerged from forty years of teaching a "religious knowledge" option. When *The Great Code* appeared, one reviewer compared it unfavorably to *Fearful Symmetry*, saying that it lacked the sense of arguments to be proved and obstacles to be overcome, and indeed the most negative reviews faulted it for being exactly what it set out to be: a teacher's book. *Anatomy of Criticism* is the book that broke the dichotomy because it sought a way that literature could be taught more deductively, as grammar is most commonly taught, with a combination of principles and examples. To date, Frye has published eleven books of criticism based on lecture series, and for each he has chosen the "classroom style," mentioned in the first, as the style he is most comfortable with (*Educated* 2).

Frye has shied away from the title of "researcher" because he has worked mainly with familiar teaching texts (*Spiritus* 3).[19] To some extent, this penchant is institutional, for at the University of Toronto, Victoria College was concerned with undergraduate education, while University College dominated graduate instruction in English. His own teachers at Victoria were old-fashioned men of learning, like Brett in philosophy; they were teachers first and then writers; their books had long gestation periods and tended to be summings up (*Spiritus* 3). Such leisure was already impossible in many universities when Frye was starting out, and he never ceases to be grateful for the time that he was given to finish his first book. Today, he laments, professors are no longer men or women of learning, but "productive scholars" (*Divisions* 103). They must hasten into print, however provisionally, with the unfortunate result that they often perish as writers and teachers in order to survive as academics. Few people in the humanities have been half as productive as Frye, but his major books have all been long in coming. Most are written from the perspective of the learned man who has knowledge to impart, yes, but reflections on that knowledge most of all. The *Anatomy* shows how literary knowledge can be ordered in the mind of a particularly learned and imaginative reader.

In the lectures given to mark Canada's centennial in 1967, Frye saw the ensuing century as belonging not only to Canada but to education. In the years to come, Frye said, the "leisure structure" of society, with the universities at the center, would play an increasingly important role in the shaping of social policy. To this extent, education could be "revolutionary" (*Modern* 89-93). These were heady words for heady times, but hardly new for Frye, whose first essay on education had appeared in a journal with strong socialist leanings, and whose *Anatomy* of a decade earlier had proposed that "the ethical purpose of a liberal education is to liberate, which can only mean to make one capable of conceiving society as free, classless, and urbane" (347).[20]   If we substitute the term "visionary education" we can see why the study of literature is central to Frye's social thought and inseparable from it. Literary works may be bound to social systems we find unacceptable, like the philosophical tyranny of Plato's *Republic* or the blood-brotherhood of D. H. Lawrence's *Women in Love*, but these very works can be liberated from their cultural limitations and brought into a redeemed city of the imagination, where no genuinely human action — word, work, or wish — is ever lost. In the sentimental education of an earlier age, the goal was to produce *simpaticos*, who would have the right feelings and the correct taste. In the visionary education, the young will see visions, the old will dream dreams, and all the Lord's people will be prophets.[21]

Because the occasion for the papers in this volume marks the thirtieth anniversary of Frye's *Anatomy*, it seems only appropriate to conclude with a Frygean version of the game of twenty questions.   If Frye's ideal education were a mode, it would be low-mimetic comedy involving actors of marriageable age, though too serious to be limited to them. If it were a symbol, its goal would be the anagogic identity where facts are released into the imagination and create the view of a classless society, a golden world that liberates even the time-bound work of literature. If it had a mythos, it would be that of spring, again associated with comedy. The exposure to great ideas throws many good students into a winter of discontent, but there usually follows a reversal of fortune as students discover their roles in the life of their times, and this recognition leads to the happy ending of spring commencement, when students are told that they will soon step into another sort of classroom, as Frye has said on at least one such occasion ("University" 83). Finally, if the visionary education had a genre, it would be the encyclopaedic treatise or anatomy, where all forms and knowledge are compatible. If all this were so, the ultimate educator would be the "theorist," in the word's etymological sense of "seer."   No responsible theorist could ignore the larger context of his theories, and so could not ignore the educational implications. For many years it has been unfashionable for theorists to address large publics, as Matthew Arnold did, but as Frye's career has progressed he has found his proper context in the global classroom.

Notes

1 Since these remarks were written, several books of related interest have appeared. Northrop Frye's *On Education* (Markham, Ont.: Fitzhenry & Whiteside, 1988) collects eighteen occasional pieces. Frye's essay *Some Reflections on Life and Habit* responds to the polemic on the closing of the American mind, to which he alluded in an earlier draft of his essay for this volume. Robert D. Denham's *Northrop Frye: An Annotated Bibliography of Primary and Secondary Sources* lists two dozen items about Frye on the subject of education. Ian Balfour's *Northrop Frye* includes a chapter on "Literature, Education, and Society" (66-77). John Ayre's *Northrop Frye: A Biography* is rarely far from education. A. C. Hamilton's *Northrop Frye: Anatomy of His Criticism* includes a section on "Literature, Criticism, and Education" (202-4), but the entire book develops the theme that Frye's criticism responds to developments in English studies at the college level. I have not drawn on these valuable books, though for ease of reference I have cited *On Education* rather than the less accessible pamphlet *On Teaching Literature*. I have reviewed the first four books for *University of Toronto Quarterly* 59 (Summer 1989), the fifth for *University of Toronto Quarterly* 60 (Summer 1990), and the sixth for the *Northrop Frye Newsletter* 3, no. 1 (1990).

2 For a thorough study of "context" in Frye's critical theory, see Denham's *Northrop Frye and Critical Method*, 132-56, 186-90; the word is also discussed in Salusinszky's essay in the present volume and in *Harper Handbook*, 122-23. (Frye did not write this entry, however). Frye's books of essays are all organized by context. For example, *The Stubborn Structure* is divided into "Contexts" and "Applications," with the first group including essays on teaching in the universities, criticism in the classroom, and the overall sequence of literary instruction.

3 Edward Weismiller, who was a Rhodes Scholar at Merton during Frye's day, returned in the late sixties to read the handwritten minutes. He told me at the time that these had all the wit and precision that readers have come to expect of Frye. Frye later told me that he had written them all at once, at the end of the year, wishing that could type them instead.

4 The question raised on the cover of the issue shows a broken bust of Frye; Stuewe's essay is entitled "Beyond Survival" in reference to Atwood's *Survival: A Thematic Guide to Canadian Literature*.

5 Frye was quoted as "a disciple of Communications Philosopher Marshall McLuhan" in the famous cover story on hippies, who reminded Frye of the "outlawed and fugitive social ideal known as the 'Land of Cockaigne,' the fairyland where all desires can be instantly gratified" ("Hippies" 20); one imagines that the reporter tried to reach McLuhan (then at Fordham) and was given Frye as the next choice. Frye has discussed McLuhanism in *The Modern Century*, chap. 1.

6 "The Case against Examinations" became an underground classic during Frye's years as principal (1959-67).

7 The combined English departments at Toronto added a dozen faculty members a year during the late sixties, and the graduate department of English added as many as sixteen new courses a year (Harris 148, 167).

8 *OED* sb. 1.4. The supplement adds the sense of a secular author's authentic works, giving as examples the Platonic and Shakespearean canons. The entry in *Harper Handbook* (88) does not accept the currently fashionable usage, though Frye did not write the entry.

9 I queried Frye on this point, and told me, in a letter of May 24, 1988, that "Bloom took the word from me, and then proceeded to apply it in a context which I had explicitly condemned." I have not found the word "canon" in Bloom's first books, *Shelley's Mythmaking* and *The Visionary Company*, though the second title implies a sort of canon. Some correspondence between Frye and Bloom has been deposited in the E. J. Pratt Library in Toronto.

10 For Frye's preface to the report, see *On Education* 46-61, and for the educational context of this report see Stamp, chap. 10: "The Liberalization of the Big Blue Schoolhouse."

11 *Literature: Uses of the Imagination* has not sold especially well, and not only because it requires coordination over several years: ironically, the books now seem to defer too much to the freewheeling sixties, especially in the choice of illustrations and of popular songs.

12 Francis Sparshott has remarked that he never heard a student ask Frye a challenging question, and never heard Frye respond directly to a challenge (148). If this was so in the fifties, it certainly was not in the seventies, when students would routinely ask quite skeptical questions, for example, about the value of myths. For some sample questions, see *On Education*, 120.

13 Frye says he taught himself to lecture without notes, so that he could be more responsive to his students ("Northrop Frye: The Better to See"). But he also tells tales of his attempts to teach out of new editions and his frustration when the pages "don't turn at the right places." His memory is more than photo-

graphic or phonographic, and seems connected to the schemas he draws on the blackboard. A longtime colleague at Victoria College says that Frye has been known to work a similar magic at meetings: he will sit and listen patiently, then say, "Look. It's like this," and draw his pattern on paper or even in chalk.

14　See *Spiritus Mundi*, 103-4, for Frye's remarks on the thesis topic; and Harris, appendix 2a for a list of Toronto PhD theses, including the thirty-one that Frye has directed. The great majority of these are studies of a single author—with several each on Blake, Yeats, and Joyce—or of two authors with a strong affinity of some sort.

15　Blake, *The Book of Urizen*, plate 2. David Cook has suggested that in writing "The Case against Locke" (in chap. 1 of *Fearful Symmetry*), Frye had to make "The Case for Locke" and "The Case against Blake," had to make the imagination more "corporeal" and Lockean than Blake saw it so that he could make Blake more acceptable to the literary academy. The argument is sufficiently interesting to warrant (if not sufficiently thorough to withstand) comparison to Salusinszky's theory of "extension" in this volume, which should be compared, in turn, to Frye's treatment of recreation in *Creation and Recreation*.

16　Frye has cited Kogan's title with some amusement (*Spiritus* 17-18).

17　See *Fearful Symmetry*, 207-35. I confess that on meeting Frye for the first time, I expected Los and found Urizen, but I was talking to him about university business.

18　See his response to the "Wright Report."

19　"I'm not a scholarly authority in any one thing," Frye told Gillian Cosgrove, adding ironically: "I'm more like the hero in Carlyle's *Sartor Resartus*: The Professor of Things in General."

20　See the entry "liberal education" in the index of the *Anatomy* for related references. "Of Liberal Education" appeared in a journal allied with the CCF, a fascinating blend of clergy, workers, and intellectuals which in time became the New Democratic Party of Canada.

21　The references are to Joel 2:28 and Numbers 11:29, two of Blake's favorite verses.

Works Cited

Applebee, Arthur N. *Tradition and Reform in the Teaching of English: A History.* Urbana: NCTE, 1974.

Atwood, Margaret. "Northrop Frye Observed." *Second Words: Selected Critical Prose.* Toronto: Anansi, 1982. 398-406.

_____. *Survival: A Thematic Guide to Canadian Literature.* Toronto: Anansi, 1972.

Ayre, John. "The Mythological Universe of Northrop Frye." *Saturday Night* 88 (May 1973): 19-24.

_____. *Northrop Frye: A Biography.* Toronto: Random House, 1989.

Balfour, Ian. *Northrop Frye.* Boston: G. K. Hall, 1988.

Bates, Ronald. "Northrop Frye, Teacher." *CEA Critic* 42 (Nov. 1979): 29-36.

Bloom, Harold. *A Map of Misreading.* New York: Oxford UP, 1975.

_____. "Reading Freud: Transference, Taboo, and Truth." *Centre and Labyrinth: Essays in Honour of Northrop Frye.* Ed. Eleanor Cook et al. Toronto: U of Toronto P, 1983. 309-28.

Cook, David. *Northrop Frye: A Vision of the New World.* New York: St. Martin's, 1985.

Cosgrove, Gillian. "Plain Mr. Frye 'Condemned to be Lonely'." *Toronto Star* 7 Aug. 1980: F1.

Denham, Robert D. *Northrop Frye: An Annotated Bibliography of Primary and Secondary Sources.* Toronto: U of Toronto P, 1987.

_____. *Northrop Frye and Critical Method.* University Park: Pennsylvania State UP, 1978.

Fite, David. *Harold Bloom: The Rhetoric of Romantic Vision.* Amherst: U of Massachusetts P, 1985.

Freedman, Adele. "The Burden of Being Northrop Frye." *Globe and Mail* 31 Oct. 1981: 21.

Frye, Northrop. *Anatomy of Criticism: Four Essays.* Princeton: Princeton UP, 1957.

_____. *The Bush Garden: Essays on the Canadian Imagination.* Toronto: Anansi, 1971.

_____. "The Case against Examinations." *Acta Victoriana* 56 (April 1932): 27-30.

_____. *Creation and Recreation.* Toronto: U of Toronto P, 1980.

_____. *The Critical Path: An Essay on the Social Context of Literary Criticism.* Bloomington: Indiana UP, 1971.

_____. "The Developing Imagination." *Learning in Language and Literature* by Northrop Frye and A. R. MacKinnon. Cambridge: Harvard UP, 1963. 31-58.

_____. *Divisions on a Ground: Essays on Canadian Culture.* Ed. James Polk. Toronto: Anansi, 1982.

_____. "Editor's Preface." *Collected Poems: E. J. Pratt.* 2nd ed. Ed. Northrop Frye. Toronto: Macmillan, 1958.

_____. *The Educated Imagination.* Toronto: CBC, 1963.

_____. *Fearful Symmetry: A Study of William Blake.* Princeton: Princeton UP, 1947; Boston: Beacon, 1962.

_____. "Foreword." *English Studies at Toronto.* By Robin S. Harris. Toronto: U of Toronto P, 1988. ix-xxi.

_____. *The Great Code: The Bible and Literature.* New York: Harcourt, 1982.

_____. *The Harper Handbook to Literature.* With Sheridan Baker and George Perkins. New York: Harper, 1985.

_____. "A Liberal Education." *Canadian Forum* 25 (1945): 134-35, 162-64.

_____. *The Modern Century.* Toronto: Oxford UP, 1967.

_____. *Northrop Frye on Shakespeare.* Ed. Robert Sandler. New Haven: Yale UP, 1986.

_____. *On Education.* Markham, Ont.: Fitzhenry & Whiteside, 1988.

_____. *On Teaching Literature.* New York: Harcourt, 1972.

_____. "Questions and Answers." *Romanticism and Contemporary Criticism.* Ed. Morris Eaves and Michael Fischer. Ithaca: Cornell UP, 1986. 29-45.

_____. "Reflections in a Mirror." *Northrop Frye in Modern Criticism: Selected Papers from the English Institute.* Ed. Murray Krieger. New York: Columbia UP, 1966.

————. *Some Reflections on Life and Habit.* Lethbridge: U of Lethbridge P, 1988.

————. *Spiritus Mundi: Essays on Literature, Myth, and Society.* Bloomington: Indiana UP, 1976.

————. *The Stubborn Structure: Essays on Criticism and Society.* Ithaca: Cornell UP, 1970.

————. "The University and the Heroic Vision." *Wascana Review* 3, no. 2 (1968): 83-87.

————. *Words with Power: A Second Study of the Bible and Literature.* New York: Harcourt, 1990.

————. "Wright Report." *Globe and Mail* 18 Mar. 1972: 6.

————, supervisory ed. *Literature: Uses of the Imagination.* 12 vols. New York: Harcourt, 1973.

Hamilton, A. C. *Northrop Frye: Anatomy of His Criticism.* Toronto: U of Toronto P, 1990.

Harcourt Brace Jovanovich. *Literature: Uses of the Imagination.* Brochure. New York: Harcourt, 1973.

Harris, Robin S. *English Studies at Toronto: A History.* Toronto: U of Toronto P, 1988.

"Hippies." *Time* 7 July 1967: 18-22.

Kogan, Pauline. *Northrop Frye: The High Priest of Clerical Obscurantism.* Montreal: Progressive Books and Periodicals, 1967.

Levin, Harry. *Why Literary Criticism Is Not an Exact Science.* Cambridge: Harvard UP, 1967.

"Northrop Frye: The Better to See." *The Graduate* 6, no. 2 (Winter 1979): 4.

Oliver, Hugh. "A Literate Person Is First and Foremost an Articulate Person." *Interchange* 7, no. 4 (1976-77): 32-38.

Reaney, James. "The Identifier Effect." *CEA Critic* 42 (Jan. 1980): 32-38.

Salusinzsky, Imre. *Criticism in Society: Interviews with Jacques Derrida, Northrop Frye, Harold Bloom, Geoffrey Hartman, Frank Kermode, Edward Said, Barbara Johnson, Frank Lentricchia, and J. Hillis Miller.* New York: Methuen, 1986.

Sparshott, Francis. "Frye in Place." *Canadian Literature* 83 (Winter 1979): 143-55.

Stamp, Robert M. *The Schools of Ontario, 1876-1976.* Toronto: U of Toronto P, 1982.

Stuewe, Paul. "Beyond Survival." *Books in Canada* 12 (Feb. 1983): 7-10.

Weston, Jessie. *From Ritual to Romance.* 1920. Garden City, NY: Doubleday, 1957.

Wolfe, Tom. "The New Life Out There." Rpt. in *McLuhan Hot and Cold.* New York: Dial, 1967. 15-34.

Essay on Frye

Hazard Adams

When first bold Norrie with his bounding mind
A work to honor William Blake designed,
He seemed a heretic to canon law,
Yet made the canon copy what he saw,
And when we youngsters to the matter came,
Will Blake and Norrie were, we found, the same.

That is the proem. I proceed now to the prose part of my anatomical poem. But I cannot pass to my real subject, which is how the science of Frye's *Anatomy* is also art, without pausing in true anatomical fashion to express my gratitude, among that of countless others, for Northrop Frye's first book, *Fearful Symmetry*, and the inspiration it gave us and still gives us after forty years.

Having said that — and it could be said about each of Frye's books as they have come out — I should like to concentrate on one point and try to clear up what I think has been a fairly widespread misunderstanding of his work, hard to eradicate because *Anatomy of Criticism* took a certain necessary shape. The misunderstanding comes from reading the polemical first chapter of the *Anatomy* and failing to notice two things: first, that as the work proceeds it turns itself outside in, appropriating a Blakean manner, the crucial point or vortex being where Frye discusses a literary form called the anatomy; second, that this turn is from declaring criticism to be a science to identifying criticism with other constitutive forms in such a way as to associate it finally with art and indeed to imply that the *Anatomy of Criticism* belongs to a literary genre that the book itself names and discusses. This move calls in question any simple difference (forgive me for introducing this word) between literature and science, raising the question of what criticism is among the human arts and sciences.

In an anatomically typical show of erudition, I should like to approach this matter via Blake. I quote first from *Jerusalem* (plate 27):

> Jerusalem the Emanation of the Giant Albion! Can it be? Is it a Truth that the Learned have explored? Was Britain the Primitive Seat of the Patriarchal Religion? If it is true, my title-page is also True, that Jerusalem was & is the Emanation of the Giant Albion. It is True and cannot be controverted.

And now from a rhetorically parallel passage in the conclusion of the *Anatomy*:

> Is literature like mathematics in being substantially useful, and not just incidentally so? That is, is it true that the verbal structures of psychology, anthropology, theology, history, law, and everything else built out of words have been informed or constructed by the same kind of myths and metaphors that we find, in their original hypothetical form, in literature?
>
> The possibility that seems to me suggested by the present discussion is as follows. (352)

There is, of course, in Frye an important difference of gesture (within the same) appropriate to a scientific style of hypothesis testing as against the stance of prophetic discovery in Blake. However, the informing myth is the same. In Blake, the primitive seat of religion is in Britain, that is, *here*; and Jerusalem in her externalized form is elsewhere or emanated from *here*. In Frye, the verbal forms of the human sciences emanate from myth and metaphor. Myth turns its inside outward to interpretive discourse. I quote from the conclusion of the *Anatomy*:

> It looks now as though Freud's view of the Oedipus complex were a psychological conception that throws some light on literary criticism. Perhaps we shall eventually decide that we have got it the wrong way round: that what happened was that the myth of Oedipus informed and gave structure to some psychological investigations at this point. (353)

One is tempted to observe that it may have looked as if Frye's notion of the archetype were a concept that throws some light on literary criticism. Perhaps we shall eventually decide that we have it the wrong way around: that what happened was that Blake's myth of Albion and Jerusalem informed and gave structure to Frye's critical investigations.

But the situation is more complicated than that. The parallel is inadequate. Freud's theory may have emanated from dream or myth, but keeps its distance, interprets, allegorizes, plays the role of Blake's great priest Urizen. It is lost from myth and claims freedom from it. Jerusalem has not just emanated from Albion, Jerusalem has changed and managed to dominate Albion by seeing him from her alien position. Frye's *Anatomy* starts out that way, sounding more like the Enion whom the pathetic Tharmas of *The Four Zoas* accuses of anatomizing him:

> Why wilt thou Examine every little fibre of my soul,
> Spreading them out before the Sun like stalks of flax to dry?
> The infant joy is beautiful, but its anatomy
> Horrible, Ghast & Deadly. Naught shalt thou find in it
> But Death, Despair & Everlasting brooding Melancholy.
> Thou wilt go mad with horror if thou dost Examine thus
> Every moment of my secret hours. (Night the First 47-53)

One must immediately observe, however, that just as Los's vision in *Jerusalem* would reintegrate Urizen, who is supreme analyst and dissecting anatomist, back into the condition of prolific Urizenizing in his concluding, albeit tentative, apocalypse. He does this by taking the "outsideness" of criticism—its aspect of externalizing science—inside by identifying his own work as an anatomy, which is one of the genres that *Anatomy of Criticism* isolates for discussion.

This having been done, we may read the "Tentative Conclusion," the rhetoric of tentativeness being a lingering aspect of scientific process, as a continuing commentary inside this particular anatomy upon itself and upon criticism. But criticism is by now not seen externally as a process of dissection, but internally as a fictive or constitutive form. The speculation on mathematics and its similarities to literature in the conclusion is not there to show that literature is mathematical or mathematics literary, but that mathematics is an art playing the role for the natural sciences that myth and literature play for the human sciences—that is, they are

different, but they are also both Albions that send forth their
Jerusalems in abstracted forms.

But Frye's critical theory is not quite one of these human sciences after all. Rather it plays a more or less mediatory role, for it
is an anatomy, which, having itself aspects of a literary genre, never
declares itself free of myth in the way that Freud's psychoanalytic
theory by implication did.

An anatomy, as the *Anatomy of Criticism* indicates, inhabits what
appears to be a curious halfway position between purely mythical
and purely mathematical poles. Or perhaps it is better characterized as curiously marginal. Yet a margin can, if grandiose enough,
be a containing circumference, the thing exiled only to be proved
central after all. A characteristic of the anatomy according to the
Anatomy of Criticism is that of the containment of a variety of
forms and genres. It may include verse, fictive and argumentative
prose, colloquy, and epistle. Frye's glossary describes it thus:

> A form of prose fiction, traditionally known as the Menippean or Varronian
> satire and represented by Burton's *Anatomy of Melancholy*, characterized by
> a great variety of subject-matter and a strong interest in ideas. In shorter
> forms it often has a *cena* or symposium setting and verse interludes. (365)

Modern anatomies have a definite tendency to foreground a
metapoetical element, that is, to be fairly forthright about com-
menting on themselves and the constitutive form that they possess.
Further, they have, as Frye points out, a cyclical form, which is, of
course, characteristic of *Anatomy of Criticism* with its great wheel
of phases.

In *Anatomy of Criticism*, Frye wakes the sleeping beauty of
romance, restoring her, if not to her medieval preeminence, at least
to the Frygean democracy of genres. At the same time, Frye
invites into the castle a creature thought by past criticism more
appropriate to the moat, the many-limbed monster of anatomy
itself. It is a curious creature which by nature turns its inside out,
its vital organs flapping in the breeze like Cuchulain in his battle
rage. Or we can say that anatomy is a genre threatening to devour
all other genres and spew them forth. But still another way to see

the anatomy is as a questioner of the division analytics, including its own: it may too easily make distinctions between genres and between literature and other constitutive forms. Frye's *Anatomy of Criticism* anatomizes criticism into its parts with great strokes of erudition and wit. It hacks up the body but it leaves a very sparse meal for the vultures because as it divides it also constitutes. This devouring, to use Blake's terms, is also prolific. That is the paradox of the anatomy as a form, and that is why the *Anatomy of Criticism* turns itself from science to art and back again. It is like the great egg of the world that Michael Robartes mentions in another modern anatomy, Yeats's *A Vision*. It manages this without breaking its shell.

At the very moment that I penned this last sentence there was a tapping at my chamber door, and there stood an old Arab tribesman who declared that he had been sent to help me complete my analytics. I thought first, this is the ghost of Yeats playing some joke at last—revenge perhaps—but I was transfixed by the Arab's opening remark and soon forgot my resentment. He said, "You should not make the other mistake that Frye's critics have made, and you are on the verge of it when you turn the *Anatomy* into art. Don't you remember that this mistake caused Frank Kermode to call the *Anatomy of Criticism* 'useless' (I employ his exact word)?" Stung by and righteously indignant at his remark because I saw that he had spied an imprecision in my discourse, I first thought to slam the door in his face. But there, the spirit of William Blake entered through my metatarsal arch. I grasped the old Arab firmly by his beard with one hand, and holding a copy of *The Critical Path* in the other, I pushed off and ascended with him to a height where I could declare that the art of the *Anatomy* was not aesthetic in the narrowly formal sense implied by Kermode's metaphysics, but like all art worthy of the name it participated "in the vision of the goal of social effort, the idea of a complete and classless civilization" (348). Thereupon my comrade, metamorphosed suddenly into a raven, croaked "never mind"; and I saw him nevermore, but found myself sitting again quietly in my study visited by a lovely yet stern muse, who whispered, "You have spoken long enough." And so, the envoi:

> When Frye declared the critic scientist
> In horror aesthetes shouted "Positivist!"
> 'Tis True, his work starts out acidulous
> And threatens us who've failed at calculus.
> But hold, anatomy's a genre with a torso
> As literary as a poem, only more so:
> Encyclopedic, episodic, long, prolific,
> In fact artistic, huge, and quite terrific.
> Now, some say art is one thing, science a shame,
> But Frye has proved them different, yet the same.

Works Cited

Frye, Northrop. *Anatomy of Criticism: Four Essays*. Princeton: Princeton UP, 1957.

————. *The Critical Path: An Essay on the Social Context of Literary Criticism*. Bloomington: Indiana UP, 1971.

————. *Fearful Symmetry: A Study of William Blake*. Princeton: Princeton UP, 1947.

Northrop Frye in a Canadian Context

David Staines

> *Hearts with one purpose alone*
> *Through summer and winter seem*
> *Enchanted to a stone*
> *To trouble the living stream. . . .*
> *Minute by minute they live;*
> *The stone's in the midst of all.*

> —W.B. Yeats, "Easter 1916"

The poet E. J. Pratt, observes Northrop Frye, "was a landmark figure in the development of the Canadian imagination. Somehow he had acquired an infallible instinct for what was central in the Canadian consciousness. . . . It's very difficult for somebody inside Canada to explain how important Pratt is to a person who has never shared the Canadian heritage" ("View" 7).

It is equally difficult for somebody inside Canada to explain to a person who has never shared the Canadian heritage how important Northrop Frye is in a Canadian context. Like Pratt, Frye is a landmark figure in the development of the Canadian imagination. For more than five decades, he has been a commentator, a caring and detached observer of the Canadian cultural, literary, and educational scenes. In these years he has published more than eighty critical essays, book reviews, introductions, and editorials that focus specifically on Canada.

And particularly since 1960, there are Frye's many books where Canada comes to play a significant role. "Canadian literature since 1960," Frye notes, "has become a real literature, and is recognized as one all over the world" (*Divisions* 30). By 1960 Canada had passed into Frye's third phase of culture, when "provincial culture becomes fully mature . . . when the artist enters into the cultural heritage that his predecessors have drawn from, and paints or writes without any sense of a criterion external to himself and his public" (*Divisions* 23). Once Canada reaches this phase, Frye's literary and social criticism never fails to include his own land in studies essentially international or nonnational.

Frye's earliest writings appeared in 1935 and 1936, and soon he would be using Canadian painting and Canadian writing as touchstones for his then tentative analyses of the structures that would be the center of his later criticism. But Canada in 1935 and 1936 was but a young literary culture. In fact, when Frye's first article in the *Canadian Forum* appeared in 1936, the journal's editor implied that a critic of Frye's perception would not devote himself to literature, for the list of contributors reads: "H. N. Frye is rapidly gaining prominence as a music critic, although at the moment he is pursuing the duties of a Fellowship in English at Victoria College" (Anon. 2).

In 1936 there were signs of a literary voice being heard in Canada: the fiction of Frederick Philip Grove and Morley Callaghan; the poetry, of course, of E. J. Pratt, who joined with five poets to produce that year a slender but significant collection titled *New Provinces*. In 1936, moreover, the *University of Toronto Quarterly*, itself founded only in 1931, initiated, under the instigation of E. K. Brown, an annual survey of Canadian letters; Brown himself conducted the annual survey of Canadian poetry until 1950, when he was succeeded, for a decade, by Frye.

Such were signs, in 1936, of a Canadian literature, but such signs were few. In the mid-thirties, Canada was still in search of writers to tell its story. "No one reads a Canadian novel unless by mistake," Douglas Bush wrote in the 1920s. "Canadian fiction never comes to grips with life, but remains weak and timid; it has nothing to say. A mass of Canadian poetry consists of apostrophes to dancing rivulets that no doubt give pleasure to the author's relatives" ("A Plea" 590). "The salvation of Canadian literature," Bush observed elsewhere, "would be a nation-wide attack of writer's cramp, lasting at least a decade. Some years spent in reading great literature of the past and present might, in the first place, cause a number of Canadian writers to desist altogether from vain wooing of the muses, which in itself would be a gain for letters and for our disappearing forests" ("Making Literature" 73).

And in the mid-thirties, no writer's cramp having occurred, the literary climate was little changed. In 1938 Frederick Philip Grove declared:

> Canadians are at bottom not interested in their own country; I honestly believe they prefer to read about dukes and lords, or about the civil war in the United States. They are supposed to be born explorers; but they have not yet heard that the human heart and soul are perhaps the only corners in this universe where unexplored and undiscovered continents are still abounding.
> This lack of mental aliveness is fundamental. Canada is a non-conductor for any sort of intellectual current. (460)

And as late as 1951, in one of his last essays before his untimely death, E. K. Brown lamented: "It is true that in most countries where criticism has flourished . . . it has found a main theme in the literature of the country where it is written. Not much of the best Canadian critical writing is on Canadian themes" ("Causerie" 17).

The exception to Brown's observation was Frye himself, who, for longer than any other commentator, in these eighty and more studies, has been exploring and explaining the environment that shaped him and that he in turn helped to shape. And he began his commentaries at a time when it was neither fashionable nor proper to study Canadian literature. Indeed in the 1930s E. K. Brown was spending some of his teaching and writing time trying to convince Canadians that American literature might have some possible validity in an English department's offerings! ("The Neglect").

While Frye's colleague Marshall McLuhan was using Canada, as he often noted, as a nineteenth-century observation post for studying or probing the modern world beyond Canada's borders, Frye himself was including his country in his writings, first in many essays and reviews that were focused specifically on Canada, and then, from the sixties to the present, in such specific studies, as well as in essays and books not specifically devoted to Canada. "I have noticed how an increasing number of writers and painters in

Canada," Frye commented in 1978, "have come to regard the place where they are living not as an accident, but as an environment that nourishes them, and which they in turn bring into articulateness" (*Divisions* 189). That observation epitomizes Frye's own relationship to his country.

From the late thirties, then, Frye has been a constant and consistent observer and commentator. As essayist and reviewer, he focused his attention steadily on the painting and the literature of his own environment. As literary editor and later editor of the *Canadian Forum*, he accepted a position to develop a major avenue for creative and critical writing. As the annual reviewer of Canadian poetry for the *University of Toronto Quarterly*, he spent the fifties, the decade of *Anatomy of Criticism*, writing detailed critiques of a prolific and important period in the development of Canadian poetry.

Although the Canadian essays and reviews contained the many ideas being worked out in a different context in the *Anatomy of Criticism*, these Canadian pieces, especially the ten long reviews for the *University of Toronto Quarterly*, have a special place in the Frye canon. The reviews, Frye admitted, proved of immense importance to him. And he took time to reflect, in the last one, on the nature of reviewing:

> The reviewer knows that he will be read by the poets, but he is not addressing them, except indirectly. It is no part of the reviewer's task to tell the poet how to write or how he should have written. . . .
>
> The reviewer's audience is the community of actual and potential readers of poetry. His task is to show what is available in poetic experience, to suggest that reading current poetry is an essential cultural activity, at least as important as keeping up with current plays or concerts or fiction. . . .
>
> The reviewer must take poetry as he finds it, must constantly struggle for the standards of good and bad in all types of poetry, must always remember that a preference for any one kind of poetry over another kind is, for him, laziness and incompetence. . . .
>
> Finally, the community that I have been addressing is the Canadian community. As Canada is a small country, that fact raises the problem: do you estimate Canadian poets in Canadian proportions or in world proportions? I have considered this question carefully, and my decision, while it may have been wrong, was deliberate. I have for the most part discussed Canadian poets as though no other contemporary poetry were available for

Canadian readers. The reviewer is not concerned with the vague relativities of "greatness," but with the positive merits of what is before him. And every genuine poet is entitled to be read with the maximum sympathy and concentration. (*Bush Garden* 124-26)

The wisdom and sanity of this reviewer's voice were almost unique in a country whose creative output was moving, again to use Frye's distinction, from writing to literature. Poets in Canada — and the number was steadily increasing — became aware of an informed critical voice whose standards were Canadian yet also international, whose knowledge was encyclopedic, and whose natural understanding of Canada was sympathetic and resonant.

Frye accepted the arduous challenge of reading all the annual publications in Canadian poetry and then writing on them, I suspect, for patriotic reasons grounded in his own university education. In describing his influential teachers at Victoria College, he once commented, "What they also had in common was a keen and generous (often very practically generous, as many could testify) interest in younger Canadian writers, and a desire to do what they could to foster the creative talent around them" (*Bush Garden* 183).

While studying Canadian writers in their own environmental context, Frye also placed them, slowly at first, but with increasing emphasis as the fifties progressed, in an international or nonnational context, the context of all literature. Frye's greatest achievement as a reviewer, for Malcolm Ross, was "to have given our writers some strong and honest assurance that they were at last out of the parish and standing with their peers on high, new ground" (173). Frye "took the writing of poetry in Canada seriously," George Johnston observes, "at a time when it was of great value to Canadian poets that someone of his stature should do so" (23). And Margaret Atwood recalls:

The only "influence" Frye had on those of us who wanted to be writers, and it was a considerable one, was to take us seriously. I'm not sure how he managed to do this, as, like most young writers, we were a pompous and self-righteous lot, but he did. In a society still largely provincial, where the practice of literature and the arts generally was regarded with a good deal of suspicion — immoral if not a frill — he made literature seem not only an honourable calling but a necessary one. . . . He always made it quite clear that it was the job of writers to write but it was certainly not the job of critics to tell them what to write. If critics ever started doing that, the writers would escape them one way or another. I've seen narrow visions of what literature ought to be produced by many writers, and even by some critics, but never by Frye. He was not prescriptive. (21)

More important, however, than the encouragement Frye offered a developing and increasingly articulate culture was his constant and consistent articulation of many of the myths of the culture itself. Canada, Frye has always insisted, haunts its writers with a nature that is Hardyesque in its bleak desolation: "Nature is seen by the poet, first as unconsciousness, then as a kind of existence which is cruel and meaningless, then as the source of the cruelty and subconscious stampedings within the human mind" (*Bush Garden* 141-42). Many of his critical observations became prophecies, as in, for example, this equally early reflection: "The poet's vision of Canada as a pioneer country to which man stands face to face with nature is bound to be superseded by a vision of Canada as a settled and civilized country, part of an international order, in which men confront the social and spiritual problems of men" (*Bush Garden* 154).

Still more important are his reiterations of unique myths that seem to haunt the Canadian imagination: the garrison mentality, that closely knit and beleaguered society at odds with its environment; the quest for the peaceable kingdom, "the haunting vision of a serenity that is both human and natural," in contrast to the horrors of the technological visions that seem embodied at times in the United States (*Bush Garden* 249); "the imaginative instability, the emotional unrest and dissatisfaction one feels about a country which has not been lived in: the tension between the mind and a surrounding not integrated with it" (*Bush Garden* 200); and, perhaps most crucially, the observation, often repeated and often pondered, that the "Canadian sensibility has been profoundly disturbed, not so much by our famous problem of identity, important as that is, as by a series of paradoxes in what confronts that identity. It is less perplexed by the question 'Who am I?' than by some such riddle as 'Where is here?'" (*Bush Garden* 220).

Frye the critic is also Frye the mythographer and mapmaker. In Canada's centennial year of 1967, he affirmed:

> The Canada to which we really do owe loyalty is the Canada that we have failed to create. In a year bound to be full of discussions of our identity, I should like to suggest that our identity, like the real identity of all nations, is the one that we have failed to achieve. It is expressed in our culture, but not attained in our life, just as Blake's new Jerusalem to be built in England's green and pleasant land is no less a genuine ideal for not having been built there. (*Modern* 122-23)

And that identity is further expressed in Frye's constant, consistent, and challenging explorations of that culture.

Finally, Frye's Canadian criticism offers an introduction to a vital and commanding literature as well as to Frye's own witty and articulate critical mind. And, typically Canadian in his avoidance of the autobiographical, Frye may offer the most accurate glimpses of himself when he writes about those Canadian artists with whom he feels a natural kinship, be they poets such as E. J. Pratt, or painters such as Lawren Harris and David Milne. In Frye's tribute to Harris, for example, he may well be presenting the ideal he himself follows. Harris was, Frye maintains, a "missionary as well as explorer: not a missionary who wants to destroy all faith that differs from his own, but a missionary who wants to make his own faith real to others. Just as a new country cannot become a civilization without explorers and pioneers going out into the loneliness of a deserted land, so no social imagination can develop except through those who have followed their own vision beyond its inevitable loneliness to its final resting place in the tradition of art" (*Bush Garden* 212).

In 1965 the *Literary History of Canada* was published, a thousand-page report on the development of Canadian literature from its earliest indications to the present. Writing the conclusion to this encyclopedic endeavor was, of course, Frye himself, and his concluding essay became an immediate classic, the single most-quoted essay in Canadian literary criticism. His overview embodied his own vision of Canada which he had been enunciating and developing for nearly three decades. As he began his conclusion, he reflected:

> Canada has produced no author who is a classic in the sense of possessing a vision greater in kind than that of his best readers (Canadians themselves might argue about one or two, but in the perspective of the world at large the statement is true). There is no Canadian writer of whom we can say what we can say of the world's major writers, that their readers can grow up inside their work without ever being aware of a circumference. (*Bush Garden* 213-14)

Whether Canada had, in 1965, produced such an author was debatable; now, more than two decades later, not a few names come to mind. But perhaps the first Canadian writer whose vision is greater in kind than that of his best readers is Northrop Frye himself.

Works Cited

Anon. *Canadian Forum* 16 (April 1936): 2.

Atwood, Margaret. "Fifties Vic." *CEA Critic* 42 (Nov. 1979): 19-22.

Brown, E. K. "Causerie." *Winnipeg Free Press* 13 Jan. 1951: 17.

_____. "The Neglect of American Literature." *Saturday Night* 47 (21 Nov. 1931): 2-3.

Bush, Douglas. "A Plea for Original Sin." *Canadian Forum* 2 (April 1922): 589-90.

_____. "Making Literature Hum." *Canadian Forum* 7 (Dec. 1926): 72-73.

Frye, Northrop. *The Bush Garden: Essays on the Canadian Imagination*. Toronto: Anansi, 1971.

_____. *Divisions on a Ground: Essays on Canadian Culture*. Toronto: Anansi, 1982.

_____. *The Modern Century*. Toronto: Oxford UP, 1967.

_____. "View of Canada: Never a Believer in a Happy Ending." *Globe and Mail* 6 Apr. 1976: 7.

Grove, Frederick Philip. "The Plight of Canadian Fiction? A Reply." *University of Toronto Quarterly* 7 (1938): 236-53.

Johnston, George. "Northrop Frye: Some Recollections and Observations." *CEA Critic* 42 (Jan. 1980): 21-25.

Ross, Malcolm. "Northrop Frye." *University of Toronto Quarterly* 41 (Winter 1972): 170-73.

Frye and Romanticism

Imre Salusinszky

If one questions the dogma that the origins of poetry are to be found in the sensibility and if one says that a fortunate poem or a fortunate painting is a synthesis of exceptional concentration . . . , we find that the operative force within us does not, in fact, seem to be the sensibility, that is to say, the feelings. It seems to be a constructive faculty, that derives its energy more from the imagination than from the sensibility.
— Wallace Stevens, "The Relations Between Poetry and Painting" (1951)

The arts, including literature, are not so much concerned with the world as it is: their concern is with the world that man is trying to build out of nature, and the imagination they appeal to is a constructive power, which is neither reason nor emotion, though including elements of both.
— Northrop Frye, "The Developing Imagination" (1963)

I

One of the things we learn from Frye is that the act of recognizing the true identity or value of any writer or text is inseparable from the act of discovering where that text or writer truly belongs. Recognition isn't a matter of isolation, but rather of typology—of *classification* in a heightened mode. So criticism will always involve the discovery of context, which will itself involve a decision about how to take a woven thing (*textus*) and weave it together (*contexere*) with other woven things. And since Frye's own practical criticism is always an inquiry into a writer or text's genuine context, we might justifiably ask: What is the context of Northrop Frye?

Now, when Frye does ask this question about other writers, his answer always turns out *not* to be the obvious one: social history. Though it is unfashionable to say so at the moment, I think that Frye is right. Social history, by itself, is too limiting a context. It fails to answer some simple but important questions: If there *is* nothing in literature which manages to transcend social history and ideology, then how is it that *The Faerie Queene* or *Paradise Lost*, for example, can still speak to us so much more forcefully and directly than, say, the *Magna Carta* or *Domesday Book*? If poetry is a history only of departed things, then why does the poetic imagination seem to have this capacity to call to us across time?

There have been several notable attempts to limit Frye himself to a historical context, seeing his kind of idealism and historical despecification as serving certain contingent bourgeois ideological needs in the fifties and sixties. Some of these attempts, like John Fekete's in *The Critical Twilight*, I find overly reductive; others, like Frank Lentricchia's in *After the New Criticism*, are powerful enough to deserve a strong answer of some kind. Such an answer would involve not denying the place of idealism and historical transcendence in Frye's work, but finding out where they come from—their context—and where they can be found in their least diluted version, which surely leads us straight to Romanticism. So my own guess, at this early stage, is that, while Frye belongs in many contexts, he belongs most truly within the history of Romanticism. This doesn't mean that I'm content merely to talk about Frye as a great critic of Romanticism, or as a great Blakean—or even as a "Romantic revivalist," the *key* figure in the overturning of the whole basket of anti-Romantic literary values which characterized the preceding Age of Eliot. Rather, I choose to talk about Frye as a *neo*-Romantic, as an extender and intensifier of the insights of English Romanticism—and therefore as a new and distinctive moment in the history of Romanticism itself.

When talking about Frye as an "extender" of Romanticism, we could probably substitute for "extension" that intellectual guerrilla tactic which Harold Bloom, in *The Anxiety of Influence*, calls "tessera"—that's the one where you read the precursor as having been definitely on the right track, but as having failed to follow it far enough (14). As you would expect, Frye's extension or tessera in respect of English Romanticism centers on the theory of imagination. Imagination is the Romantic faculty proper; though not—so this argument goes—as proper as in neo-Romanticism. Frye's own theory of imagination can be shown to have a complicated and revisionary relation to all of the major English Romantic writers.

Most importantly, Frye works a revision upon Wordsworth and Coleridge in that he sees imagination as a constructive, unifying and originating faculty, rather than as a perceptive or reproductive one. Wordsworth and Coleridge retain too many vestiges of "naturalism" to satisfy Frye. When he relegates Coleridge and Wordsworth to a pre-Blakean tradition of "critical naturalism" (*Fables* 30), I take it that he means by "naturalism" what Blake means in his annotations when he calls attention to the vestiges of natural religion in Wordsworth (782, 784). For Blake or Frye, the Wordsworthian relation between mind and nature as mutual supremacy or interchangeable domination simply fails to go far enough. In Frye's account, the imagination "swallows" reality; and, as he says in *The Educated Imagination*, it won't stop until it's swallowed everything (80).

In order to bring Frye's notion of imagination into focus as a neo-Romanticism, we should recall the cardinal organizing concept of *Anatomy of Criticism* and much of Frye's subsequent work: the idea that the existing monuments of literature do not comprise a set of discrete fragments spread out across time, but rather make up a "self-contained literary universe" or "order of words" spread out in conceptual space (350, 17). Now, it is not enough to say that we need a certain kind of imagination in order to be able to view this construct: it's much truer to say that the literary universe and the imagination are, in fact, one. Blake believed that God and the imagination were identical and, as Frye is always reminding us, the only God Blake could believe in was an incarnate God. Well, the point is that the neo-Romantic does not believe in "pure" or "abstract" imagination any more than Blake could believe in a removed or abstracted God. The neo-Romantic imagination must be, at least potentially, an incarnate imagination. Once we have identified the imagination with the literary universe or order of words, we see that the literary universe and, therefore, the imagination become incarnate in all of the individual works of literature.

The genealogy of this idea is pervasively Romantic. It construes poetry not as a discrete set of accounts or descriptions or responses to the historical world, but as a vast visionary analogue to that world — one which threatens constantly to take it over or "swallow" it. The impulse behind such a way of thinking about things is broadly Wordsworthian: it is deductive, unifying, and, above all, holistic. But Frye's account of the literary universe is far more complete and explicit than anything we actually get in Romanticism. There is, of course, a latent version of it in Blake, for whom each new poem is neither original, nor an imitation of some preexistent world, but rather a borrowing or displacement (to use the Frygean term) of a story or archetype already present within the archives of Los, the unfallen artist. Every age, says Blake in *Jerusalem*, "renews its powers from these Works / With every pathetic story possible to happen from Hate or / Wayward Love . . . ." (638). There is an even stronger hint of the idea in Shelley, in that famous passage of the *Defence* where he speaks of "that great poem, which all poets, like the cooperating thoughts of one great mind, have built up since the beginning of the world" (7: 124).

There is no exact equivalent to this that comes to mind in Wordsworth, but Coleridge provides a fascinating case. The furtive idea of "poetry" as a larger construct, a literary universe containing all existent and possible poems, haunts the pages of the *Biographia*. No one has ever known quite what to make of Coleridge's distinction between "poem" and "poetry" in Chapter XIV of the *Biographia* — where he says bafflingly that a poem of any length "neither can be, nor ought to be, all poetry" (173) — and this might be because not even Coleridge is quite aware of the truth he's on the verge of discovering. He certainly makes an explicit identification between "poetry" and "imagination," since "poetry" is precisely what takes place whenever the "synthetic and magical power" operates (174). But the extension which I would try to work upon Coleridge, reading him through Frye, becomes more plausible if we take it that Coleridge is using "poetry" in anything like a consistent way when, back in Chapter I, he reminisces about his former schoolmaster in these terms:

> I learnt from him that poetry, even that of the loftiest and, seemingly, that of the wildest odes, had a logic of its own as severe as that of science; and more difficult, because more subtle, more complex, and dependent on more and more fugitive causes. (3)

A logic of its own as severe as that of science? Frye, in a 1964 essay on teaching and scholarship, says of his own literary universe that it is a "coherent field of study which trains the imagination quite as systematically and efficiently as the sciences train the reason" (*Stubborn* 102). The whole of *Anatomy* is in a very real sense about the power of imagination, through something like Coleridgean "poetry," to provide linkages or extensities between poems—thus forming larger configurations out of them—rather than simply essences or intensities within poems: its ability, in a word, to invoke the incarnation of the whole literary system through the poem.

What enables the kind of mapping of a literary universe performed by Frye in the *Anatomy* and elsewhere is a radical identification between poetry (or imagination) and nature. This identification is also made, constantly and explicitly, by Blake; and implicitly (though pejoratively) by Schiller, in *Naive and Sentimental Poetry*, when he says that sentimental poets seek nature, but naive poets are nature (106). But the identification is held in suspension by Wordsworth and Coleridge, which may be why, as has often enough been noticed, Coleridge wavers between two conceptions of imagination. On the one hand, there is the "Kubla Khan" vision of an all-embracing power which is able to spin reality out of the bowels of its own imaginings, and which Coleridge will sometimes advocate unreservedly as a kind of metafaculty, as when he hopes to "be able to evolve all the five senses, that is, to deduce them from *one sense*" (*Collected Letters* 2: 706). On the other hand, there is that lesser "mediatory power" (*Collected Works* 6: 29) which must share the powers of the mind with "reason" and "understanding" (*Biographia* 113). It is out of this second, accommodated Romanticism that all of those Eolian harps, fading coals, correspondent breezes, and auxiliary lights emerge: Romantic tropes for an imagination which requires some inspiring agency external to itself.

This is the side of High Romanticism fixed upon by Northrop Frye, who depicts Coleridge's theory of imagination as ambivalent and insufficient—as shot through with "critical naturalism," and a dose of New Criticism to boot. In his 1961 essay on "Myth, Fiction and Displacement," Frye remarks that Coleridge

> does not really think of imagination as a constructive power at all. He means by imagination what we have called the reproductive power, the ability to bring to life the texture of characterization and imagery. (*Fables* 30)

Frye's strong revision of Coleridge's notion of imagination emerges in a distinction between "sense" and "vision," which is drawn in a 1962 essay called "The Imaginative and the Imaginary," and in a whole series of other texts in the sixties. Sense is the attitude with which the scientist confronts nature; it involves the recognition of "things as they are"; it tells us "what kind of reality the imagination must found itself on." Vision, on the other hand, is based not on recognition but on desire; it works towards a mental construct of the world mankind "wants to live in." Sense and vision, we are told, comprise the two "opposite and complementary forces" within imagination (*Fables* 151-53).

This distinction between sense and vision is obviously related, or relatable, to Coleridge's distinction in the *Biographia* between a perceptive primary imagination and a recreative secondary imagination "differing only in degree" from it (167). But Frye manages a strong swerve away from Coleridge, and this consists in the priority which vision, in his version of the story, has over sense—a priority indicated by his remark in a 1958 lecture that it is through the *literary* imagination that "modern man participates in society" ("Humanities" 19). Frye's revision of Coleridge here executes a reversal: Coleridge finds in the secondary imagination an "echo" of the primary; "vision," however, is the *least* displaced of Frye's

two poles, and it is in the poetic imagination that Frye would find
what Coleridge locates in the perceptive or primary imagination:
"a repetition in the finite mind of the eternal act of creation in the
infinite I AM" (*Biographia* 167). Vision is primary, which is why
"reality is primarily what we create, not what we contemplate"
(*Stubborn Structure* 51). In neo-Romanticism, then, the poetic
imagination is no longer seen (to borrow Coleridge's terms) as dis-
solving or diffusing or dissipating, but rather as creating and con-
structing reality in its own right.

II

Having outlined some of the ways in which Frye can be seen as a
neo-Romantic, I now want to broaden the argument and start
thinking about the possibility of a neo-Romantic *movement* in
North American writing over the last half-century or so. Of course,
a literary movement needs to be founded on artists as well as critics, and here we should note the remarkable connections between
Frye's work and the poetry and criticism of the modern poet who
has interested and influenced him most over the years: Wallace
Stevens. Stevens, like Frye, places imagination above reason and
emotion as "the sum of our faculties" (*Necessary* 61). In the
Anatomy, Frye says that humanity imposes imaginative structures
on nature, and seeks to identify the human with the nonhuman,
through a drive which he simply calls "desire" (106)—the desire to
turn an "environment" into a "home." This corresponds exactly
to what Stevens calls the "rage for order," a rage born out of the
fact "that we live in a place / That is not our own and, much more,
not ourselves" (*Collected* 130, 383). For Frye, as we have seen,
the imagination "swallows" reality. Riffling through Stevens's
"Adagia" commonplace book—perhaps the richest source of con-
densed poetic wisdom since Blake's "Proverbs of Hell"—we discover that "the imagination consumes and exhausts some element
of reality," and that "the imagination is man's power over nature"
(*Opus* 173, 179). In an essay of 1941, Stevens says that the poet
must "abstract reality, which he does by placing it in his imagina-

tion" (*Necessary* 23). In *The Educated Imagination*, Frye says that although the world created by the imagination looks like a dream, it isn't: "It's the real world, the real form of human society hidden behind the one we see" (152). There is, says Stevens, "a world of poetry indistinguishable from the world in which we live, or . . . from the world in which we shall come to live" (*Necessary* 31). According to him, "we live in a world of the imagination, in which reality and contact with it are the great blessings" (*Letters* 753).

If Stevens and Frye could be woven together as members of a neo-Romantic movement, it might not be too fanciful to think of a "second generation" of neo-Romantics coming after them. In other words, there might be an actual thematic basis for the indisputable fact that Frye and Stevens were the critic and poet who exercised the greatest influence over the younger North American critics and poets of the fifties and sixties. We can readily see the sort of "community of spirit" that exists between Frye and Stevens reproduced, in the second generation, by two of their most distinguished progeny: Harold Bloom and John Ashbery.

One objection which can immediately be made to this kind of schematic argument is that Frye was born a whole generation — thirty-three years — after Stevens. But here we are assisted by Stevens's late development, by subsequent creative longevity, and by the fact that his more "theoretical" writings were all produced towards the end of his life. *Transport to Summer*, which includes "Notes toward a Supreme Fiction," was published in 1947, the same year as *Fearful Symmetry*. Stevens's essays are likewise products of the forties — so that hardly a decade separates the two accounts of imagination as "constructive power" quoted at the head of this essay. And Stevens's last poems — *The Auroras of Autumn* and "The Rock" — are works of the same decade as *Anatomy of Criticism*.

As Frye himself acknowledges, Stevens has "turned up constantly" in his writing (*Spiritus* vii), and in fact Frye has been one of the key figures in the critical canonization of Stevens. This was a task which Frye turned to immediately upon completing the *Anatomy*, writing his first essay on Stevens, "The Realistic Oriole," at Indiana University in the summer of 1956. So Frye went straight to Stevens in composing the "complementary volume concerned with practical criticism" projected in the preface to *Anatomy* (vii). It was a relatively early moment to declare that Stevens is "not one of our expendable rhetoricians, but one of our small handful of essential poets" (*Fables* 255).

In the course of a conversation about Stevens in 1982, Frye told me that he became fascinated with Stevens as a teenager, working in the Moncton Public Library. His first contact with Stevens came through Louis Untermeyer's anthology of *Modern American Poetry* (1921), which included "To the One of Fictive Music" ("Unreal, give back to us what once you gave: / The imagination that we spurned and crave" [331; *Collected* 88]). Frye did eventually meet Stevens, just once. In 1948, he heard Stevens deliver his extraordinary lecture on "Imagination as Value" at an English Institute meeting at Columbia University. It is the lecture where Stevens says that "the great poems of heaven and hell have been written and the great poem of the earth remains to be written"; that the value of imagination "is the value of the way of thinking by which we project the idea of God into the idea of man"; and where he closes by asking: "Of what value is anything to the solitary and those that live in misery and terror, except the imagination?" (*Necessary* 142, 150, 155).

After the talk, the young author of *Fearful Symmetry* was taken up to meet the distinguished speaker. Predictably, the encounter between these two unusually reserved men did not turn out to be one of the great literary meetings: Stevens spent the whole time asking Frye about various stockbrokers and insurance people he had met on his one visit to Toronto—nine years before Frye was born.

There can be no doubt, though, about the similarities between, and the shared Romantic heritage of, Frye's "literary universe" or "order of words" and what Stevens called the "supreme fiction" or "poem of the whole." Like the literary universe, the supreme fiction carries an apocalyptic and revelatory message. Stevens says that his work is about "the possibility of a supreme fiction, recog-

nized as a fiction, in which men could propose to themselves a ful-
filment" (*Letters* 820). And like Frye, Stevens sees his own
supreme fiction as containing a *secular* revelation: "The relation of
art to life is of the first importance in a skeptical age since, in the
absence of a belief in God, the mind turns to its own creations and
examines them, not alone from the aesthetic point of view, but for
what they reveal, for what they validate and invalidate, for the support that they give" (*Opus* 159).

Certainly, Stevens's supreme fiction or "endlessly elaborating
poem" (*Collected* 486) is the closest *poetic* analogue to Frye's
vision of a literary universe since the Shelleyan "great poem" on
which poets have been working since the beginning of the world.
In the supreme fiction we get precisely that Fryean sense of a vast,
composite poem, the contours of which could be potentially
mapped out. In a late poem called "A Primitive Like an
Orb"—which Frye would have first encountered around the time
that he was beginning *Anatomy*—Stevens writes that

> The central poem is the poem of the whole,
> The poem of the composition of the whole . . .
> And the miraculous multiplex of lesser poems,
> Not merely into a whole, but a poem of
> The whole, the essential compact of the parts. (*Collected* 442)

An "orb," according to the *OED*, is a circle, disk, sphere, or even
an "organized or collective whole." The last is related to an
unusual verbal usage: to gather or enclose. Circularity, organized
wholeness, the ability to enclose: these are all qualities of the literary universe as well as of the supreme fiction. "Primitive Like an
Orb" outlines the same encroachments of imagination upon reality
that we have discerned in Frye: "It is / As if the central poem
became the world, / And the world the central poem" (*Collected*
441). ("The great conquest," says Stevens in the "Adagia," "is the
conquest of reality" [*Opus* 168].)

To suggest the nature of the relationship between the "central
poem" and the "miraculous multiplex of lesser poems," Stevens has
constant recourse to a figure we have already noted in Frye. In

"Notes toward a Supreme Fiction," there is a very clear sense of the individual poem as on the one hand unique and holistic, but on the other hand as *incarnating* a larger, less definable poem:

Is there a poem that never reaches words

And one that chaffers the time away?
Is the poem both peculiar and general?
There's a meditation there, in which there seems

To be an evasion, a thing not apprehended or
Not apprehended well. (*Collected* 396)

The incarnation motif is developed slightly later in "A Primitive Like an Orb." The "general" poem is an unfillable category, and evades proper definition:

We do not prove the existence of the poem.
It is something seen and known in lesser poems.
It is the huge, high harmony that sounds
A little and a little, suddenly,
By means of a separate sense. (*Collected* 440)

So a "separate sense" is required to bring the "general poem" even partly into view, and this sense I take to be the imagination. As well as an understanding of "poetry" as something capable of incarnation through individual poems, what Stevens also has is a Frygean sense of "poetry" as something equivalent to imagination. The imagination and the supreme fiction are, as it happens, also, one. Stevens writes to Hi Simons in 1940: "Poetry is the spirit, as the poem is the body. Crudely stated, poetry is the imagination" (*Letters* 363). It is not exactly the deified Romantic imagination, but rather "poetry" in this special sense, that the neo-Romantics worship:

If one no longer believes in God (as truth), it is not possible merely to disbe-lieve; it becomes necessary to believe in something else. Logically, I ought to believe in essential imagination, but that has its difficulties. It is easier to believe in a thing created by the imagination. A good deal of my poetry recently has concerned an identity for that thing. (*Letters* 370)

So Stevens can't believe in "essential" or "abstracted" imagination any more than Frye can. His imagination must be, at least potentially, incarnate, and he approaches this through an identification between imagination and a sense of "poetry" as a vast, composite structure. The "difficulties" mentioned in Stevens's letter are anxieties occasioned by the burdens of tradition: the Romantics had *already* transferred belief onto "essential imagination," and Stevens was a strong enough imaginative figure to need to choose to believe the fiction that he himself had created whatever fictions he chose to believe in.

The parallels which I have been drawing between Stevens and Frye, and the talk of a neo-Romantic movement, make it sound as if I want to return to a historical context for Frye, after disparaging that notion at the outset. However, I think that we can stay within *literary* history when looking for the reason why, at this particular time, both Stevens and Frye should have turned to Romanticism and attempted a revitalized version of it. In both cases, this turn has less to do with a particular moment in the crises of monopoly capitalism than with a reaction against the anti-Romanticism of the literary movement immediately preceding: the High Modernism of the School of Eliot. We should never allow Frye's irenic tone to lead us to underestimate the extent to which his ideas and program have been framed in direct opposition to everything Eliot stood for. At the beginning of *Spiritus Mundi*, in an essay of 1973, Frye says that reading Eliot's *After Strange Gods* was one of the things that turned him towards the study of Blake: "I felt that I could hardly get interested in any poet who was not closer to being the opposite in all respects to what Eliot thought he was" (14).

"Eliot and I are dead opposites," writes Stevens in a letter of 1950: "I have been doing about everything that he would not be likely to do" (677). In fact, there are veiled and semiveiled barbs against Eliot and Pound throughout Stevens's letters, and in particular on the issue of their anti-Romanticism. People, he says in a 1935 letter, tend to think in batches:

> The predominating batch today seems to think that the romantic as we know
> it is the slightest possible aspect of the thing. The English feel as badly about
> the romantic as they do about the sentimental. (282)

There is plenty of evidence to suggest that Stevens, as well as
Blake, has always functioned as a "dead opposite" to Eliot in Frye's
mind. In an uncollected essay of 1959, "Religion and Modern
Poetry," Frye says that in Eliot and poets like him,

> the religious feeling is intensely Catholic in the sense that the sacramental life
> initiated by the Church is the informing power of ordinary life. Protestantism
> has had practically no direct influence on modern poetry. In the Romantics,
> however, for whom the artist is a creator, participating in the creative energy
> of God, there is a natural analogy with Protestant religious experience. (34)

At the end of the essay, though, Frye says that, the "sacramental
poets" notwithstanding, the sense of the "divinity of the imagination" is not extinct among modern poets. His chief instance of the
Romantic survival is Stevens. He finds that Stevens's poetry moved
towards a "curious wistfulness," leading Frye to wonder "whether
poetry may not be doing its greatest service to religion by following
its own bent for uninhibited imaginative speculation" (36).

III

I spoke earlier about an identification between poetry and nature,
drawn by Blake, Schiller, and Frye. It is an identification also made
by Stevens, powerfully:

> I want, as poet, to be that in nature, which constitutes nature's very self. I
> want to be nature in the form of a man, with all the resources of nature.
> (*Letters* 790)

A kind of logical corollary to the nature/poetry identification will
be a consequent elevation of criticism. Everyone, as it were, takes
a step forward, and the deification of criticism becomes the neo-
Romantic equivalent of High-Romantic poet-worship, where critics
are to poetry what poets were to nature. Where the literary uni-

verse is viewed as a distinct and, indeed, ideal realm, the critic who
is possessed of the visionary faculty required to perceive and communicate it will assume a sacramental function. In neo-Romanticism, the prophetic power of Shelley's Prometheus is extended
from poet to critic, who now also lifts a veil from in front of reality.
In other words, the redemptive properties which the Romantics
ascribed to the poetic imagination now become qualities of the
critical imagination as well. This is why Frye can talk about literature in *The Educated Imagination* as a "human apocalypse, man's
revelation to man," and about criticism as "not a body of adjudica-
tions, but the awareness of that revelation, the last judgement of
mankind" (105). For a poet, Stevens also had an incredibly elevated view of criticism, or at least of a potential criticism. He wrote
in a letter of 1954 that it was of the "utmost interest" to him to "try
to find out whether it is possible to formulate a theory of poetry
that would make poetry a significant humanity of such a nature and
scope that it could be established as a normal, vital field of study
for all comers" (853) — which happens to be a wonderfully concise
statement of the central aims of the project called *Anatomy of
Criticism.*

In the *Anatomy*, Frye talks a great deal about *dianoia*: the
theme, idea, or argument of a poem. *Dianoia* comes to us as a
simultaneous mental grasp of what a poem means; it occurs outside
time, when we experience the full significance of the poem as a
pattern spread out in mental space. One of Frye's achievements
has been to rejuvenate interest in poetic thought or argument,
after the New Critical privileging of texture and form. In "The
Realistic Oriole," Frye says that Stevens, like Blake, is an
"admirable poet in whom to study the processes of poetic thought
at work," and contrasts him on precisely these grounds to Eliot
(*Fables* 238-39) Poetic argument may well be the quality that distinguishes an "essential poet" from an "expendable rhetorician."
As for Stevens himself, he wrote in a 1936 letter that to combine
the "pleasure of poetry" with the "pleasure of thought" was "one
of the jobs that lies ahead" (312). Through *dianoia*, we can at last

connect Frye properly with Wordsworth, too, because the flash of instantaneous comprehension unlimited by time—which is how Frye talks about *dianoia*—is precisely the Wordsworthian epiphanic moment; the moment in which time, the body, and the ego are all laid asleep, and we see into the life of things.

Now, criticism as a whole has precisely this relation to the whole of literature—to the poem of the whole. As total *dianoia*, criticism is the sole enabling activity which can provide an anagogy or "leading up" to the order of words, supreme fiction, or imaginative world. This must surely be why so much of *Anatomy's* Polemical Introduction is taken up with establishing criticism's independence, its precious freedom from "enclosure movements" and "external invasions" from related disciplines and various religio-historical determinisms (6-7).

This brings us back to the opening question of whether history can provide a sufficient and final context for literature: neo-Romanticism, like Romanticism before it, is a denial, for better or worse, of precisely that. I say "for better or worse" because adherents to any version of Romanticism, perhaps now more than ever, get caught up in a perpetual cycle of crises of conscience regarding their historical responsibilities. Every time we attach ourselves to Shelley's article of faith—that poets are the unacknowledged legislators of the world—some skeptical soul is likely to be on hand to remind us that a much better example of that phenomenon would be Colonel Oliver North. At present, a particular kind of historicism represents the most formidable enclosure movement advancing upon criticism from outside—if there is really an outside. Here are some lines from near the end of the *Anatomy*:

> The imaginative element in works of art . . . lifts them clear of the bondage of history. Anything that emerges from the total experience of criticism to form part of a liberal education becomes, by virtue of that fact, part of the emancipated and humane community of culture, whatever its original reference. Thus liberal education liberates the works of culture themselves as well as the mind they educate. The corruption out of which human art has been constructed will always remain in the art, but the imaginative quality of the art preserves it in its corruption, like the corpse of a saint. (347-48)

Given the current dialectics of criticism—where an old-fashioned historical determinism and a new-fashioned Foucauldian pessimism combine to make the literary tradition look suspiciously like a history of bad faith—these words about the escape from historical context are, for me, the words which most powerfully escape *Anatomy's* own historical context. Back in 1957, there might have seemed to be an evasion about them, a thing not apprehended or not apprehended well. But across these three decades—now that we've learned to "reread" the poets as such preeminent reservoirs of misogyny, misanthropy, and mystification—the lines would seem to issue a direct call. They even sound like prophecy, leading us to suspect that the *Anatomy* has waited until its thirtieth birthday before assuming its full ministry.

Works Cited

Blake, William. *Complete Writings*. Ed. Geoffrey Keynes. London: Oxford UP, 1966.

Bloom, Harold. *The Anxiety of Influence*. New York, Oxford UP, 1973.

Coleridge, Samuel Taylor. *Biographia Literaria or Biographical Sketches of My Literary Life and Opinions*. Ed. George Watson. London: Dent, 1965.

————. *Collected Letters of Samuel Taylor Coleridge*. Ed. Earl Leslie Griggs. 6 vols. Oxford: Oxford UP, 1956.

————. *The Collected Works of Samuel Taylor Coleridge*. Ed. Kathleen Coburn. London: Routledge, 1969 –.

Fekete, John. *The Critical Twilight: Explorations in the Ideology of Anglo-American Literary Theory from Eliot to McLuhan*. London: Routledge, 1977.

Frye, Northrop. *Anatomy of Criticism: Four Essays*. Princeton: Princeton UP, 1957.

————. *The Educated Imagination*. Bloomington: Indiana UP, 1963.

————. *Fables of Identity: Studies in Poetic Mythology*. New York: Harcourt, 1963.

————. "Humanities in a New World." *3 Lectures*. Toronto: U of Toronto P, 1958. 9-23.

_____. "Religion and Modern Poetry." *Challenge and Response: Modern Ideas and Religion.* Ed. R. C. Chalmers and John A. Irving. Toronto: Ryerson, 1959. 23-36.

_____. *Spiritus Mundi: Essays on Literature, Myth, and Society.* Bloomington: Indiana UP, 1976.

_____. *The Stubborn Structure: Essays on Criticism and Society.* London: Methuen, 1970.

Lentricchia, Frank. *After the New Criticism.* Chicago: U of Chicago P, 1980.

Schiller, Friedrich. *Naive and Sentimental Poetry and On the Sublime.* Trans. Julius A. Elias. New York: Ungar, 1966.

Shelley, Percy Bysshe. *The Complete Works of Percy Bysshe Shelley.* Ed. Robert Ingpen and Walter E. Peck. 10 vols. London: Ernest Benn, 1926-30.

Stevens, Wallace. *Collected Poems.* 1954. London: Faber, 1971.

_____. *Letters of Wallace Stevens.* Ed. Holly Stevens. 1966. London: Faber, 1967.

_____. *The Necessary Angel: Essays on Reality and Imagination.* New York: Knopf, 1951.

_____. *Opus Posthumous.* Ed. Samuel French Morse. New York: Knopf, 1957.

Untermeyer, Louis. *Modern American Poetry.* London: Jonathan Cape, 1925.

II. *Anatomy of Criticism* in Retrospect

Auguries of Influence

Robert D. Denham

One could hardly have predicted from the early reviews of *Anatomy of Criticism* that twenty-five years after its publication it would become the most frequently cited book in the arts and humanities written by a twentieth-century author (Garfield, "Most Cited"). This is not to say that all of the reviewers were caught napping. David Daiches called the *Anatomy* "brilliant" and "provocative." "It is the rare kind of book," he said, "that the reader must come to terms with, even if it takes him the rest of his life" (69, 72) Hilary Corke regarded the book "as one of the very few important critical productions" of his time (80). Harold Bloom saw the *Anatomy* as a work of "an imagination whose power and discipline are unique in contemporary criticism," adding that the book would "be widely read and used" (130, 133). G. L. Anderson called the book a "monumental work" (18). And Hazard Adams saw the publication of the *Anatomy* as "an event of real importance and excitement" (533). But by and large most of the reviewers — and even Frye himself — seemed not to sense that the *Anatomy* would come to command the extraordinary attention it in fact received in the decades that followed.[1] It did not take long, however, for the discussions of Frye's work to start pouring forth. Beginning in the late 1960s and continuing through the 1970s, commentaries on his writing appeared at the rate of more than twenty a year, most of the assessments having been spawned by the *Anatomy*. And even though Frye had ten books to his credit a decade after the *Anatomy* was published,[2] his considerable reputation and influence during the sixties and seventies were clearly rooted in the principles developed in that book.

Two decades ago it was, therefore, easy to speak of Frye's influence. Writing in 1970, Walter Jackson Bate regarded Frye as "probably the most influential critic writing in English since the 1950s" (xiv-xv); and a few years before, Murray Krieger had remarked that Frye had "had an influence—indeed an absolute hold—on a generation of developing literary critics greater and more exclusive than that of any one theorist in recent critical history" (1). But what is Frye's status as we move into the last decade of the century?

In the early 1960s Frye was selected by the Committee on Research Activities of the Modern Language Association to write the chapter on literary criticism for the MLA pamphlet *The Aims and Methods of Scholarship in Modern Languages and Literatures* (Thorpe). Twenty years later, Lawrence Lipking wrote a new version on the same topic. He begins his chapter by calling attention to four cardinal points in Frye's earlier piece and then contends that each of them seems, two decades later, to be quaintly archaic. Lipking does refer to Frye's earlier essay as "brilliant" (79), and he says that "Frye's principles retain their interest; they have been debated but not refuted" (80). But it is clear that for Lipking the current practice of criticism has moved on to matters different from those that concerned Frye. "Just as the history of recent criticism," says Lipking, "might be dubbed, from the perspective of twenty years ago, 'the return to fallacies,' doubtless many positions that seem fallacious today are awaiting their moment of return" (81). The possibility of a return implies, of course, a disappearance. But while it is clear that from the perspective of poststructuralism Frye's project lies at the fringe of its various agendas, it is no less clear, I believe, that Frye's influence has not in recent years waned. The question, at any rate, is worth pursuing.

I begin with a review of some of the quantitative indexes that might serve as auguries of Frye's influence. From an international point of view, one measure of Frye's status is the degree to which his work has moved beyond the boundaries of the Anglo-American community. Italy and Japan provide perhaps the best examples. After his three-week lecture tour of Italy in 1979, Frye said, "There is more interest in my work in Italy than anywhere else in the world" (French 15). This is surely an overstatement, yet more of Frye's books have been translated into Italian—thirteen altogether, with another in progress—than in any other language. Seven of his books have been translated into Japanese, and the translation of at least one additional book—*The Great Code*—is underway in Japan. Of the twenty-six books Frye has written, all but seven either have been or shortly will be translated, making a total of forty-six translations in nine languages. In addition to Italian and Japanese, one can read Frye's books in French, Spanish, German, Portuguese, Serbo-Croatian, Romanian, and Dutch, and new translations are underway in Hungarian. His essays can also be read in Polish and Turkish. Among the translated books, all but three have appeared since 1969 (twenty-two years after *Fearful Symmetry* was published), and during the last decade the rate of progression of all this translating activity has been more than arithmetic. Although many of those whose native tongue is not English read Frye's work in the original, this flurry of translation suggests that Frye has a large and growing readership abroad.

In Europe, where the media take intellectuals more seriously, Frye was practically lionized during the 1979 lecture tour of Italy. The occasion was not well reported in the Canadian press, and it gained no attention at all in this country. But his presence in Italy received front-page coverage in newspapers from both the right and the left, he was interviewed in Rome on prime-time national television, and he received standing ovations for his lectures on Castiglione. The Italian media had a similar reaction to the international congress devoted to Frye's work in May 1987, when more than a half-dozen of the major newspapers covered the congress, and reporters jostled to interview him throughout the three-day event. The published accounts of this gathering, where twenty-six scholars read papers about Frye's work, make for a rather thick file.[3] In this country we are not accustomed to a literary critic being given such attention, but elsewhere, including, of course, Frye's native Canada, a large number of people regard Northrop Frye as a cultural hero of the highest order.

Another augury of influence is the large body of secondary literature that has grown up around Frye's work. The books, essays, reviews, dissertations, and articles devoted in whole or major part to his criticism now number more than 1900 items, and if one charts the historical contours of this secondary literature, there is no indication that the interest in his critical theory has at all diminished during the past two decades. One might reply, then, to Terry Eagleton's recent rhetorical question, "Who now reads Frye?"[4] by saying, "A considerable number." Of the eleven books devoted exclusively to Frye's criticism, nine have been published since 1978; since 1985, more than 170 articles or parts of books have been devoted to his work; and *The Great Code*, which was published in 1982 and is already available in fifteen different editions and translations, has been the subject of at least five symposia and has been reviewed in more than 160 journals and magazines, a number that continues to grow as the reviews of the translations of the book appear. The first dissertation on Frye's work was written in 1963. Now there are forty-six devoted in whole or major part to his thought. Thus, while the interest in archetypal criticism has clearly abated since the 1960s, Frye's work continues to occasion a flood of commentary each year — and it originates not just in this country. Frye's Italian bibliography now numbers more than 150 items. Moreover, two major books on Frye have recently appeared: John Ayre's *Northrop Frye: A Biography* was published in 1989, and A. C. Hamilton's comprehensive study, *Northrop Frye: Anatomy of His Criticism*, in 1990.

Another quantitative index of a writer's influence is the frequency with which his or her writings are cited by others, and Frye's work has entered into the common currency of critical exchange as much as that of any other literary critic. In the late 1970s Frye was among the eight most frequently cited writers not just in literary criticism but in the arts and humanities generally. (Those who ranked ahead of Frye were Marx, Aristotle, Shakespeare, Lenin, Plato, Freud, and Barthes.)[5] An updated version of the citation data in 1986 reveals that Kant, Hegel, Cicero, and Chomsky have made their way onto the most-cited list, but Frye is still there, the third most frequently cited writer in the arts and humanities born in the twentieth century (Garfield, "The 250 Most-Cited Authors").

In *After the New Criticism* Frank Lentricchia notes that William Wimsatt's attack on Frye at the 1965 English Institute was "an effort to forestall the elevation of Frye to critical sainthood." Lentricchia then records his opinion that, as it turned out,

> canonization was not imminent after all. Eulogy—or perhaps its ritual opposite, the debunking of the recently deceased, recently mythologized hero—was more properly in order. For the English Institute volume of 1966 reads now, with the hindsight a decade provides, like an ironic memorial... to a critical career that had reached stardom and then, more quickly than anyone might have predicted in the middle 1960s, lost its claim to center stage .... Frye... was unceremoniously tossed 'on the dump' with other useless relics. (30)[6]

Although Frye would abjure all talk of canonization and stardom, he did have this to say in a 1990 interview: "I'm often described as somebody who is now in the past and whose reputation has collapsed, but I don't think I'm any further down skid row than the deconstructionists are" (Caley).[7] The citation indexes and other bibliographic records provide evidence to confirm his judgment.

By "bibliographic records" I refer, on the one hand, to the writings of those theorists, such as Lentricchia himself, who have felt compelled to come to terms with Frye's work, even when they disagree with him. These include—to name only some of the most visible—Harold Bloom, Hayden White, Geoffrey Hartman, Murray Krieger, Jonathan Culler, Tzvetan Todorov, Paul Ricoeur, Terry Eagleton, Angus Fletcher, Paul Hernadi, Frank Kermode, Fredric Jameson, Robert Scholes, W. K. Wimsatt, Jr., and René Wellek. I refer, on the other hand, to the massive body of practical criticism Frye's theories have engendered.[8] Frye has clearly altered the way a whole generation of critics have talked about literary structure. The *Anatomy* appeared at the time when the New Criticism was at its height, and it is hardly possible, after the *Anatomy*, to define literary form solely in terms of poetic texture. More than any other critic Frye has shown us that literature is indeed made out of other literature, and that we miss a great deal if we neglect the recurring narrative patterns and images in the literary tradition. No one has yet systematically charted Frye's influence on applied criticism, but the *Arts and Humanities Citation Index* testifies convincingly that *Anatomy of Criticism* has become a twentieth-century *Poetics* — an indispensable guidebook for hundreds of essays in practical criticism. It has provided countless critics a method, a system of terms, and a conceptual framework for their commentaries on individual literary works.

It is commonplace for those in Blake studies to remark that *Fearful Symmetry* revolutionized our understanding of the prophetic books. Joseph Natoli's bibliography, *Twentieth-century Blake Criticism*, is subtitled "Northrop Frye to the Present," and Natoli notes that *Fearful Symmetry* is "the work which has inspired a twentieth-century . . . exhaustive, academic study of Blake" (ix). In Shakespearean studies, we are just beginning to realize the important impact that Frye's work has had, especially what he has written about the comedies and romances. Several surveys of Shakespearean criticism make this clear. Robert Merrill, for example, sees the development of the generic approach to Shakespearean comedy as beginning with *Anatomy of Criticism* and *A Natural Perspective*, books that chart an entirely new direction for Shakespearean criticism. He notes that what the works of eight major Shakespeareans have in common is that they all respond to, clarify, or expand some aspect of Frye's ideas about comic form. Similarly, in a long review-article, Wayne Rebhorn sets out to determine the impact of Frye's work on the interpretation of the comedies and romances since the early 1960s. After examining the work of dozens of Shakespeareans, he concludes that Frye's criticism of the comedies provides the starting point for almost all subsequent criticism. Later work depends directly on Frye, or else it complements, qualifies, or deepens his theories. Two other Shakespeareans — Lawrence Danson and R. S. White — have come to quite similar conclusions.

A thinker's influence can be measured, too, by the degree to which his or her ideas spill over into other disciplines. This kind of influence is much more common in the continental than in the

Anglo-American tradition, where the subject matter for critics, at least until recently, has very seldom gone beyond literature in any extensive way. But when one sees philosophers (such as Robert Nozick) and historians (such as Hayden White) and psychologists (such as Roy Schafer) and legal theorists (such as Robin West) and Biblical critics of all persuasions begin to draw on Frye's ideas, one begins to suspect that his work might be an exception to the insularity of Anglo-American criticism, at least as we know it in this century. Even the art of nursing has drawn upon Frye's theories of interpretation for models of diagnosis and care (Hagey). In these respects, the critics Frye most resembles in stature and influence are Coleridge and Arnold, both of whom had very large visions of the critic's task.

Frye's influence rests in no small measure, to be sure, upon *Anatomy of Criticism*, but it certainly rests upon a great deal more than that book. His first substantial essays—on music and film and ballet and opera and painting—appeared in the early 1930s. Six decades is a long time to have been writing criticism, and an extraordinarily large stream of it has poured from Frye's pen. In addition to the twenty-six books, Frye has edited another fifteen, and his own bibliography contains now more than six hundred items: essays, reviews, contributions to books, interviews, sermons, sound recordings, films, videotapes, and the like. Add to this the unpublished writing and one has a body of work that is approaching epic proportions.[9] One cannot have an epic without size, which is one of the reasons I have briefly reviewed the volume of writing in the Frye canon and the secondary literature it has occasioned. But what accounts for Frye's influence finally is not the number of bookshelves his work fills but its encyclopedic range, its continuous vision, and rhetorical power. Let me indicate what I mean by each of these three things.

By "encyclopedic range" I mean that Frye has taken as his subject matter the entire body of Western literature and criticism—from Homer to Thomas Pynchon, from the Bible to Giorgio Bassani, from Shakespeare and Milton to Margaret Atwood and Irving Layton, from Plato and Aristotle to Dickinson and Eliot, from

Dante and Castiglione to Joyce and Stevens. But I also mean that Frye has gone beyond things strictly literary to engage the whole range of artistic, philosophical, educational, political, social, religious, and cultural issues that confront us in the modern century. A number of his early essays and reviews, as just said, were not on literary topics at all. The index to his bibliography reveals that there are as many essays on education as there are on Blake. He has written on Vico and Spengler, Langer and Eliade, Freud and Jung, Cassirer and Frazer, Machiavelli and Marx, Thomas More and Castiglione, Wagner and William Morris, Toynbee and Niebuhr, and, of course, the Bible. He has written on contemporary youth culture, the law, history, communications theory, utopias and social contract theories, science, television, and Canadian social and political issues of all sorts. Large portions of *Spiritus Mundi, The Stubborn Structure, Divisions on a Ground, The Modern Century, Northrop Frye on Culture and Literature, Myth and Metaphor,* and *Reading the World* are devoted to matters not strictly literary. These books were all published after 1970. Yet the centrifugal movement in Frye's work has been present from the beginning. On the basis of the *Anatomy* Frye is sometimes caricatured as a purely formal theorist, or else as one interested primarily in producing ingenious literary taxonomies. But even in the *Anatomy,* the most formally imposing of his books and one that argues throughout for the autonomy of literature, the broader social direction that criticism for Frye must ultimately take forms a strong bass note throughout.

The most important of Frye's essays in social and cultural criticism is, I think, *The Critical Path* (1971), a book that stands as a good example of the centrifugal direction that he sees criticism as necessarily taking. The process of interpreting the social myths of culture, he says in this book, is "very similar to criticism in literature," adding that "different forms of critical interpretation cannot be sharply separated, whether they are applied to the plays of Shakespeare, the manuscripts of the Bible, the American Constitution, or the oral traditions of an aboriginal tribe. In the area of general concern they converge, however widely the technical contexts in law, theology, literature or anthropology may differ" (123). In other words, while literary critics are not qualified to handle all the "technical contexts" of culture, there is no reason for them to back away from the cultural phenomena that form the social environment of literature. "The modern critic," Frye says in *The Critical Path*, "is a student of mythology, and his total subject embraces not merely literature, but the areas of concern which the mythical language of belief enters and informs. These areas constitute the mythological subjects, and they include large parts of religion, philosophy, political theory, and the social sciences" (98). Eleanor Cook and her colleagues remark in the introduction to the *Festschrift* honoring Frye that for him "it is true both that literary criticism should be based upon 'what the whole of literature actually does' and that literature as a whole reflects an organized myth of human experience" (viii). The critical path in Frye's case turns out, then, to be a broad thoroughfare, and his expansive conception of criticism, rooted in his ideas about this "organized myth of human experience," is, I believe, one of the chief reasons for his staying power.

Frye's views on this organized myth spring from a number of his fundamental assumptions—the priority of the imagination to nature and history, the priority of likeness to difference, the priority of the metaphoric uses of language to its metonymic and descriptive uses, the priority of mythology (or primary concern) to ideology (or secondary concern), the priority of unity to diversity. These commitments are present in Frye's work almost from the beginning, or at least from the 1940s and 1950s when he was writing, practically side by side, *Fearful Symmetry* and *Anatomy of Criticism*.[10] In a time when the careers of many critics seem to follow the ups and downs of critical fashion there is, perhaps, a virtue in continuity. For those, like Lentricchia, who see Frye's work as a "useless relic," it is worth observing that the Frye canon is not yet complete. Ten of his books have appeared in the last decade. In addition, since 1980 Frye has written more than seventy additional pieces, of which a good two dozen can be called major. While there have been differing emphases throughout the six decades of

Frye's writing career, the continuity of the vision of culture and criticism that emerges from his large body of work is, it seems to me, unequalled in the Anglo-American tradition.

The vision first recorded in *Fearful Symmetry* and continued in the *Anatomy* comes full circle, as Ian Balfour has recently argued, in *The Great Code*. Those familiar with this last book will recognize the following passages:

> The Bible is . . . the archetype of Western culture, and the Bible, with its derivatives, provides the basis for most of our major art: for Dante, Milton, Michelangelo, Raphael, Bach, the great cathedrals, and so on. The most complete form of art is a cyclic vision, which, like the Bible, sees the world between the two poles of fall and redemption.

> We reach final understanding of the Bible when our imaginations become possessed by the Jesus of the resurrection, the pure community of a divine Man, the absolute civilization of the city of God.

> In pursuing the meaning of a word in poetry we follow the course of the meaning of the word "word" itself, which signifies the unit of meaning, the Scripture, and the Son of God and Man.

> A genuine higher criticism of the Bible . . . would be a synthesizing process which would start with the assumption that the Bible is a definitive myth, a single archetypal structure extending from creation to apocalypse. Its heuristic principle would be St. Augustine's axiom that the Old Testament is revealed in the New and the New concealed in the Old: that the two testaments are not so much allegories of one another as metaphorical identifications of one another. We cannot trace the Bible back, even historically, to a time when its materials were not being shaped into a typological unity. . . . This is the only way in which we can deal with the Bible as the major informing influence on literary symbolism which it actually has been.

> The Bible as a whole . . . presents a gigantic cycle from creation to apocalypse, within which is the heroic quest of the Messiah from incarnation to apotheosis.

In these five passages we have some of the fundamental assumptions upon which *The Great Code* is based: Frye's premise of the cyclic vision of the Bible, his theory of imaginative possession, his understanding of literal meaning, his view that literature is made out of other literature, and his conception of the Bible as the definitive mythical, archetypal, and typological structure in our heritage. The five quotations come, however, not from *The Great Code*, although one could find quite similar passages in that book. They come rather from *Fearful Symmetry* and *Anatomy of Criticism*, and they thus illustrate how radically central the Bible has been in Frye's vision of both literature and criticism from the beginning.[11]

Throughout the chapters on myth, metaphor, imagery, and rhetoric in *The Great Code* runs Frye's fundamental assumption — that the interpretation of the Bible requires that it be seen as a unity, that it must be read in terms of its beginning and end, that it does possess a total structure. Present also are a number of Frye's other fundamental *literary* assumptions, methods, and principles: his notion of literal meaning, his synchronic and diachronic perspectives, his idea of the conventional structure of imagery, his centripetal method of reading, his conception of radical metaphor, and the like — all of which would serve to illuminate, if followed through, the continuity of Frye's critical vision.

Frye is a schematic thinker, one who always arranges his categories in spatially diagrammatic ways. But it can be argued, I believe, that in addition to the *dianoia* or spatial structure in Frye's work, there is a *mythos* or temporal structure as well — that it follows something like the spiral design of which M. H. Abrams speaks in *Natural Supernaturalism*, where the process of continuity-in-change is used to describe the work of a series of poets who circle back to where they began, except that their truths, once Unity is regained, exist on a higher conceptual level. Such a pattern, from Unity to Multiplicity and back to Unity, describes the pattern of Frye's own career. He keeps circling back to the same issues because his vision of literature and life is a continuous one. "I don't think I can say a great deal more within the category of literature," Frye confessed a few years ago, "which is not repeating what I have already said. Everybody is born with a certain number of ideas built into him — like ova for females — and you have only a certain amount. Beyond that you're repeating yourself" (Freedman). There is a great deal to be said for the singular, discrete, discontinuous insight, whether poetic or critical. There is a great deal more to be said, I believe, for the plural, comprehensive, continuous vision, and this is the second main reason that Frye continues to be read.

Since the time of Horace we have customarily spoken of literature within the framework of a series of bipolar categories: *res* and *verba*, content and form, substance and style, the *utile* and the *dulce*, instruction and delight. These categories are not, of course, restricted to the criticism of belles lettres: they can be applied to texts of any kind. Very few of Frye's readers have been able to speak of his work without referring to the second of these categories, which is what I meant by saying that Frye's criticism has endured because of its rhetorical power. Some critical discourse rests upon things other than its explanatory power and discursive good sense. Frye himself has pointed out that the Nobel Prize Committee, in excluding criticism from the genres of literature, has missed the mark a bit in defining its ground rules. "The real function of literary scholarship and criticism," he says, "is so little understood, even by those who practise it, that it is hard not to think of it, even yet, as somehow sub-creative, in contrast to the 'creative' writing of poems and novels, as though creativity were an attribute of those genres rather than of the people using them" (*Spiritus* 105). In short, the qualities of Frye's style are qualities we associate with the charm of rhetorical and poetic creativity. A number of critics have been great writers. Plato, Nietzsche, Sartre, and Rousseau come to mind. I believe that Frye is in the tradition of these critics because he writes with wit, elegance, and a sense of aesthetic form. His prose style is aphoristic and epigrammatic; frequently dependent upon the sentence, rather than the paragraph, to carry it along; and often oracular. Despite its effort to sustain lengthy and complex arguments, Frye's prose is filled with the qualities we associate with the charm of rhetorical creativity and the power of poetic metaphor. "I am a critic," he says, "who thinks as poets think. That's what, if you like, makes me distinctive as a critic. I don't say that there aren't other critics who think metaphorically, but I do; and I think that whatever success I have as a critic I have because I can speak the language of metaphor with less of an accent" (Cayley).

To put it another way, we can say that Frye's writing has all of the characteristics of what he calls the anatomy—that form of prose fiction that is extroverted, intellectual, often satiric, born of a thematic interest, replete with catalogues and diagrams, encyclopedic in scope, and reliant on the free play of intellectual fancy. Like its forerunner, the Menippean satire, it presents us, Frye says, "with a vision of the world in terms of a single intellectual pattern" (*Anatomy* 310)—a description that could well characterize Frye's own *Anatomy of Criticism*, as Hazard Adams points out in his "Essay on Frye" in this volume. A book with its own oracular rhythm, associational logic, cyclical and epicyclical designs, the *Anatomy* is, in part at least, a narrative to unravel and a design to contemplate—as are many of Frye's other works, including *The Great Code*. "Anatomies," he says in the introduction to that book, "have an extraordinary pulling power" (xxi). Frye holds the Blakean view that the imagination is both a perceptive and a constructive faculty, and that design is a structural principle in the arts. It is a structural principle in his criticism as well, and part of the attraction he holds for his readers comes from the imaginative structure of his discourse.[12]

In predicting the fate of any writer—poet or critic—one cannot help but be reminded of the caveats in *Anatomy of Criticism* about the fragility of our judgments. Time will tell. But time has already told us a great deal about the durability of Frye's work, and as we move toward the twenty-first century it does seem clear, contrary to the opinions of the critical avant-garde, that Frye continues to speak with authority to a wide range of readers. The essays by Hayden White, Patricia Parker, and Paul Hernadi that follow in this section suggest quite eloquently that Frye's work does indeed continue to speak to critics in a poststructuralist age—critics of quite different persuasion. The span of Frye's career has carried him through the old New Criticism and into the new New Criticism, and for forty years his influence has been large, I believe, because his work is larger than either. "The great—and increasingly needed — value of Frye's work," remarks Frank McConnell, "is that it not so much bridges the gap between New Critical formalism and poststructuralism as strikes precisely the right, human balance between them" (625).

Influence is not without anxieties, as Harold Bloom reminds us. Perhaps we should let Bloom, who has himself frequently felt the burden of the past in Frye's presence behind him, have the final word on the auguries of influence:

> Frye is surely the major critic in the English language. Now that I am mature and willing to face my indebtedness, Northrop Frye does seem to me — for all my complaints about his idealization and his authentic Platonism and his authentic Christianity — a kind of Miltonic figure. He is certainly the largest and most crucial literary critic since the divine Walter and the divine Oscar: he really is that good. (62)

Notes

1 "For a theoretical book bristling with terminology," Frye says, "the *Anatomy* has acquired an unexpectedly wide audience" ("Critical Theory" 14). More than eighty reviews of the *Anatomy* were published. The briefest and surely the most curious review was written by Florence Hill Morris, who, after advising the readers of her column on "Fireside Gardening" to "pore through books of the subject" of foliage and flower arrangement, proceeds to annotate a list of such books. Included among them is *Anatomy of Criticism* [!], the complete annotation for which is this: "A difficult book to read, but with study the material is most helpful." However baffling we might find the juxtaposition of the *Anatomy* and green-thumb manuals, Ms. Morris's thirteen-word judgment does stand as a rather fit abstract for many of the reviews that appeared outside of gardening columns.

2 *Fearful Symmetry* (1947), *Anatomy of Criticism* (1957), *The Educated Imagination* (1963), *Fables of Identity* (1963), *T. S. Eliot* (1963), *The Well-Tempered Critic* (1963), *A Natural Perspective* (1965), *The Return of Eden* (1965), *Fools of Time* (1967), and *The Modern Century* (1967).

3 For the Italian reports on the conference, which was called "Convegno Internazionale: Ritratto di Northrop Frye," see Carboni, d'Amico, Fabre, Gebbia, Mussapi, and Placido. See also the articles on Frye by Alessandro Gebbia, Piero Boitani, Baldo Meo, and Agostino Lombardo in *MondOperaio* 40 (June 1987): 100-17.

4 As quoted by Kahan (3). In *Literary Theory* Eagleton remarks that "Northrop Frye and the New Critics thought they had pulled off a synthesis of the two [liberal humanism and structuralism], but how many students of literature today read them? Liberal humanism has dwindled to the impotent conscience of bourgeois society, gentle, sensitive, and ineffectual; structuralism has already more or less vanished into the literary museum" (199).

5 The citation data are for the years 1978-79. They are compiled from the first two annual editions of the *Arts and Humanities Citation Index* (*A&HCI*), which represent about 150,000 items in approximately 1,000 journals containing more than 900,000 citations from periodical literature. See Garfield, "Most Cited" and "Is Information." Since 1979 the *A&HCI* contains citations in books as well. Combined data from the *Social Sciences Citation Index*, which began publication in 1966, and the *A&HCI*, which began in 1975,

reveal that the *Anatomy* has been cited in more than 1,045 publications. See "This Week's Citation Classic," *Current Contents* 5 (30 Jan. 1989): 14.

6 In 1987, Lentricchia reports that what he was trying to do in *After the New Criticism* was "to point up the structuralist and poststructuralist moment already in Frye," and he expresses concern that the critical avant-garde has either forgotten Frye's work or pretended that it didn't exist (Salusinszky 185-86). One is hard pressed, however, to discover these ideas in Lentricchia's earlier critique.

7 Cf. Frye's remark in 1983: "I am feeling out of the great critical trends today. I'm totally out of fashion, and I think I'm rather relieved to be" (Bogdan 266). A large number of Frye's readers, however, seem not to be interested in fashion.

8 For a fairly complete account of the literature about Frye's work, see Denham and the updates that appear in the *Northrop Frye Newsletter*.

9 According to Robert Brandeis, the "Northrop Frye Collection at Victoria University Library [University of Toronto] is the most comprehensive collection of manuscripts, typescripts, and correspondence in existence in an academic institution," occupying more than ten meters of shelf space ("Northrop Frye: An Exhibition" 1).

10 Although ten years separate the publication dates of the two books, Frye published fourteen articles between 1942 and 1955 that were incorporated into *Anatomy of Criticism*.

11 The passages are from *Fearful Symmetry* 109-10, 389, 428, and *Anatomy of Criticism* 315-316.

12 The best account of the foundations of the creative appeal in Frye's work is the essay by Bert O. States, "Northrop Frye and the Anatomy of Wit."

Works Cited

Abrams, M. H. *Natural Supernaturalism*. New York: Norton, 1971.

Adams, Hazard. Review of *Anatomy of Criticism*. *Journal of Aesthetics and Art Criticism* 16 (June 1958): 533-34.

Anderson, G. L. Review of *Anatomy of Criticism*. *Seventeenth-Century News* 16 (Summer 1958): 17-18.

Ayre, John. *Northrop Frye: A Critical Biography*. Toronto: Random House, 1989.

Balfour, Ian. *Northrop Frye*. Boston: Twayne, 1988.

Bate, Walter Jackson. *Criticism: The Major Texts*. Enl. ed. New York: Harcourt, 1970.

Bloom, Harold. "Harold Bloom" [interview]. *Criticism in Society* by Imre Salusinszky. New York: Methuen, 1987. 45-73.

Bloom, Harold. "A New Poetics." *Yale Review* 47 (Sept. 1957): 130-33.

Bogdan, Deanne. "Moncton, Mentors, and Memories: An Interview with Northrop Frye." *Studies in Canadian Literature* 11 (Fall 1986): 246-69.

Brandeis, Robert. "Northrop Frye: An Exhibition." E. J. Pratt Library, Victoria University, [1989].

Caley, David. "The Ideas of Northrop Frye." CBC Audiotape: Program broadcast on CBC Radio's Ideas series, Feb. 19, Feb., 26, and Mar. 5, 1990. Toronto: CBC, 1990.

Carboni, Guido. "Northrop Frye tra Alice e Dio." *Il Manifesto* 29 May 1987: 10.

Cook, Eleanor, et al., ed. *Centre and Labyrinth: Essays in Honour of Northrop Frye.* Toronto: U of Toronto P, 1983.

Corke, Hilary. "Sweeping the Interpreter's House." *Encounter* 10 (Feb. 1958): 79-82.

Daiches, David. Review of *Anatomy of Criticism. Modern Philology* 56 (Aug. 1958): 69-72.

d'Amico, Masolino. "Frye: 'Dall'ironia al mito'." *La Stampa* 28 May 1987: 3.

Danson, Lawrence. "Twentieth-Century Shakespeare Criticism: The Comedies." *The Cambridge Companion to Shakespeare Studies.* Ed. Stanley Wells. Cambridge: Cambridge UP, 1986. 231-39.

Denham, Robert D. *Northrop Frye: An Annotated Bibliography of Primary and Secondary Sources.* Toronto: U of Toronto P, 1987.

Eagelton, Terry. *Literary Theory: An Introduction.* Minneapolis: U of Minnesota P, 1983.

Fabre, Giorgio. "Freddo come Frye." *Roma* 27 May 1987: 23.

Freedman, Adele. "The Burden of Being Northrop Frye." *Globe and Mail* 3 Oct. 1981: E1.

French, William. "Frye the Conqueror Wows Them in Italy." *Globe and Mail* 14 June 1979: 15.

Frye, Northrop. *Anatomy of Criticism: Four Essays.* Princeton: Princeton UP, 1957.

_____. *The Critical Path: As Essay on the Social Context of Literary Criticism.* Bloomington: Indiana UP, 1971.

_____. "Critical Theory: Structure, Archetypes, and the Order of Words." *Current Contents* 5 (30 Jan. 1989): 14.

_____. *Divisions on a Ground: Essays on Canadian Culture.* Ed. James Polk. Toronto: Anansi, 1982.

_____. *The Educated Imagination.* Bloomington: Indiana UP, 1964.

_____. *Fables of Identity: Studies in Poetic Mythology.* New York: Harcourt, 1963.

_____. *Fearful Symmetry: A Study of William Blake.* Princeton: Princeton UP, 1947.

_____. *Fools of Time: Studies in Shakespearean Tragedy.* Toronto: U of Toronto P, 1967.

_____. *The Great Code: The Bible and Literature.* New York: Harcourt, 1982.

_____. *The Modern Century.* Toronto: Oxford UP, 1967.

_____. *Myth and Metaphor: Selected Essays, 1974-1988.* Ed. Robert D. Denham. Charlottesville: UP of Virginia, 1990.

_____. *A Natural Perspective: The Development of Shakespearean Comedy and Romance.* New York: Columbia UP, 1965.

_____. *Northrop Frye on Culture and Literature: A Collection of Review Essays,* ed. Robert D. Denham. Chicago: U of Chicago P, 1978.

_____. *Reading the World: Selected Writings, 1935-1976.* Ed. Robert D. Denham. New York: Peter Lang, 1990.

_____. *The Return of Eden: Five Essays on Milton's Epics.* Toronto: U of Toronto P, 1965.

_____. *Spiritus Mundi: Essays on Literature, Myth, and Society.* Bloomington: Indiana UP, 1976.

_____. *T. S. Eliot.* Edinburgh: Oliver and Boyd, 1963.

_____. *The Well-Tempered Critic.* Bloomington: Indiana UP, 1963.

Garfield, Eugene. "Is Information Retrieval in the Arts and Humanities Inherently Different from that in Science? The Effect that ISI's Citation Index for the Arts and Humanities Is Expected to Have on Future Scholarship." *Library Quarterly* 50 (1980): 40-57.

_____. "Most-Cited Authors in the Arts and Humanities, 1977-78." *Current Contents* 32 (6 Aug. 1979): 5-10; rpt. in Garfield, *Essays of an Information Scientist.* Vol. 4. Philadelphia: ISI Press, 1981. 238-43.

_____. "The 250 Most-Cited Authors in the *Arts & Humanities Citation Index,* 1976-1983." *Current Contents* 48 (1 Dec. 1986): 3-10.

Gebbia, Alessandro. "Osmosi tra le storie culturale e sociale." *Avanti!* 7 Mar. 1987.

Hagey, Rebecca. "Codes and Coping: A Nursing Tribute to Northrop Frye." *Nursing Papers/Perspectives en nursing* 16 (Summer 1984): 13-39

Hamilton, A.C. *Northrop Frye: Anatomy of His Criticism.* Toronto: U of Toronto Press, 1990.

Kahan, Marcia. "Pillow Talk." *Books in Canada* 14 (April 1985): 3-4.

Krieger, Murray. "Northrop Frye and Contemporary Criticism." *Northrop Frye in Modern Criticism.* Ed. Murray Krieger. New York: Columbia UP, 1966.

Lentricchia, Frank. *After the New Criticism.* Chicago: U of Chicago P, 1980.

Lipking, Lawrence. "Literary Criticism." *Introduction to Scholarship in Modern Languages and Literatures.* Ed. Joseph Gibaldi. New York: Modern Language Association, 1981. 79-97.

McConnell, Frank. "Northrop Frye and *Anatomy of Criticism.*" *Sewanee Review* 92 (Fall 1984): 622-29.

Merrill, Robert. "The Generic Approach in Recent Criticism of Shakespeare's Comedies and Romances." *Texas Studies in Language and Literature* 20 (Fall 1978): 474-87.

Morris, Florence Hill. "Fireside Gardening." *Augusta Chronicle* [Georgia] 26 Nov. 1967.

Mussapi, Roberto. "Frye: lo scrittore e figlio de scrittori." *Il Giornale* 27 May 1987: 3.

Natoli, Joseph. *Twentieth-century Blake Criticism: Northrop Frye to the Present.* New York: Garland, 1982.

Northrop Frye Newsletter 1 (Fall 1988) —. Copies available from the editor, English Department, Roanoke College, Salem, VA 24253.

Nozick, Robert. *Philosophical Explanations.* Cambridge: Harvard UP, 1981.

Placido, Beniamino. "La spada di carta." *La Repubblica* 29 May 1987: 24-25.

Rebhorn, Wayne A. "After Frye: A Review Article on the Interpretation of Shakespearean Comedy and Romance." *Texas Studies in Language and Literature* 21 (Winter 1979): 553-82.

Salusinszky, Imre. "Frank Lentricchia" [interview]. *Criticism in Society.* New York: Methuen, 1987. 177-206.

Schafer, Roy. *A New Language for Psychoanalysis.* New Haven: Yale UP, 1976. 22-56.

States, Bert O. "Northrop Frye and the Anatomy of Wit." *Hudson Review* (Autumn 1988): 457-79.

"This Week's Citation Classic." *Current Contents* 5 (30 Jan. 1989): 14.

Thorpe, James, ed. *The Aims and Methods of Scholarship in Modern Languages and Literatures.* New York: Modern Language Association, 1963.

West, Robin. "Jurisprudence as Narrative." *New York University Law Review* 60 (May 1985): 145-211.

White, Hayden. "The Fictions of Factual Representations." *The Literature of Fact: Selected Papers from the English Institute.* Ed. Angus Fletcher. New York: Columbia UP, 1976.

_____. "Getting out of History." *Diacritics* 12 (Fall 1982): 2-13.

_____. "The Historical Text as Literary Artifact." *Clio* 3 (June 1974): 277-303.

_____. "Interpretation in History." *New Literary History* 4 (Winter 1973): 281-314.

_____. *Metahistory.* Baltimore: Johns Hopkins UP, 1973.

_____. "The Structure of Historical Narrative." *Clio* 1 (June 1972): 5-20.

White, R. S. "Criticism of the Comedies up to *The Merchant of Venice.*" *Shakespeare Survey* 37 (1984): 2-3.

Wimsatt, W. K., Jr. "Northrop Frye: Criticism as Myth." *Northrop Frye in Modern Criticism.* Ed. Murray Krieger. New York: Columbia UP, 1966. 75-107.

Ideology and Counterideology
in the *Anatomy*

Hayden White

The principal charge of ideological contamination leveled against Frye's *Anatomy of Criticism* by such critics as Terry Eagleton, Frank Lentricchia, and Fredric Jameson turns upon the question of its formalist—structuralist or protostructuralist, by which is meant its intrinsically ahistorical—orientation. Here "ideology" consists of a certain blindness to the true nature of the relation between "literature" and "history," a tendency to repress the awareness of "history" conceived as "social reality" and to displace this awareness onto some level or dimension of human consciousness—such as religion, spirit, or consciousness itself—which will be treated as the "substance" of "literature" such that "literature's" meaning will be conceived to reside therein rather than in its relation to "history," conceived as the ultimate determining instance of what every aspect of "culture" must finally be about.

But, of course, Frye's *Anatomy* contains what amounts to a philosophy of history. It directly confronts the question of what a distinctively "historical criticism" might or should consist of. It explicitly distinguishes "historical criticism" from "ethical," "archetypal," and "rhetorical" criticism. And it directly addresses the question of the kind of theory that must inform a specifically "historical" criticism or, to put it in somewhat different terms, what a "historically self-conscious" criticism might or should consist of.

By way of considering the "ideology" of Frye's *Anatomy*—and what I conceive to be its implicit or inherently counterideological element—I want to reflect on the "First Essay" in the *Anatomy*, the section of the work entitled "Historical Criticism: Theory of Modes." The question that interests me is this: If, among other things, the ideology of any given notion of criticism can be said to reside in its denial, repression, or sublimation of a consciousness of "history," wherein does such denial, repression, or sublimation consist in the *Anatomy*? The "First Essay" suggests that "Historical Criticism" is a necessary element of criticism in general; indeed, by the very placement of this topic as the "first" essay, the *Anatomy* suggests that "historical criticism" is primary, perhaps even foundational to the whole literary critical enterprise; that, indeed, the distinctive natures of the other kinds of criticism— ethical, archetypal, and rhetorical—can be comprehended in terms of the differences between them and a criticism distinctively historical in nature. So that it might be thought: what the *Anatomy* projects in the "modes" of ethical, archetypal, and rhetorical criticism can be comprehended in terms of their differences from the *historical* mode.

As thus envisaged, and insofar as ideology would be understood as a specifically ahistorical mode of criticism, it would seem that the *Anatomy* provides some insight into the specifically ideological (insofar as they are contrasted more or less explicitly with the historical mode of criticism) aspects of ethical, archetypal, and rhetorical criticism. These latter would be ideological precisely insofar as they represent a different modality, a specifically ahistorical modality, of critical address. For which limitation, which ideological and ideologizing limitation, the historical mode would serve as a corrective, a specifically "counterideological" corrective—given the fact that, from a certain perspective, e.g., that represented by critical theorists such as Eagleton, Jameson, and Lentricchia, the principal corrective to an ideological perspective on literary history is provided only by a distinctively "historical" perspective on "history" itself. But if "history" is the corrective of ideology, what is meant by "history"? And more pertinently, what is meant by historical consciousness or—more commonsensically—a historical perspective on literature?

Here we must confront directly the implications of the strangely reticent, certainly ambiguous, title of the "First Essay," namely, "Historical Criticism: Theory of Modes." The title of this essay suggests some crucial relation between a specifically "historical" mode of criticism, a critical practice launched from within a specifically "historical" perspective (as against those of "ethical," "archetypal," and "rhetorical" criticisms), and a (or some) "theory of modes." Just as ethical criticism presupposes a theory of symbols, archetypal criticism a theory of myths, and rhetorical criticism a theory of genres, so "historical criticism" presupposes a (or some) "theory of modes."

On the face of it, the relation indicated by the colon (that at once joins and disjoins "Historical Criticism" and "Theory of Modes") is more striking than the other couples designating the relation of a critical practice (ethical, archetypal, rhetorical) to a general *kind* of theory (of symbols, of myths, and of genres respectively). The coupling of the practice of historical criticism with a (or some) theory of modes is striking (puzzling, provocative), because we do not normally think of a distinctively historical consciousness as being characterized by (informed by, governed by, determined by) a theory of *modes*. Historical inquiry, analysis, and reflection is usually thought to be informed either by no "theory" at all (the empiricist illusion), or by some general notion (a loose theoretical perspective) of the nature of the relation of events to their social contexts, the point of view indicated by the term "contexualism." Historians conventionally deal with events (small-scale or large-scale) and the relations of events to their social contexts (small-scale or large-scale). Historical criticism deals with such "events" as texts, corpora, canons, traditions, genres, authors, audiences, and so on, and seeks to relate them to their contexts (more or less extensive in space and time). What Frye suggests in the *Anatomy* is that the categories relevant to the characterization and analysis of such relationships are those that derive from our notions of "modality" rather than those of either "quantity" (unity, plurality, totality), "quality" (reality, negation, limitation), or "relation" (inherence and subsistence, causality and dependence, activity and passivity) — to use Kant's proposed classification of the species of categories set forth in his first *Critique*. Recall Kant's definition of the fourfold nature of the "judgments of taste" in the third *Critique*: as to quality: the judgment of the beautiful is "disinterested"; as to quantity: it pleases universally without requiring a concept; as to relationship: it apprehends a nonpurposive purposiveness; as to modality (of satisfaction): the beautiful is that which, without any concept is cognized as the object of a *necessary* satisfaction. The categories proper to our apprehension of "modal" relationships are, in Kant's view, those of "possibility-impossibility," "existence-nonexistence," and "necessity-contingency."

Now, these categories are, I submit, precisely those that predominate in any specifically *historical* apprehension of reality — whether historians, individually or as a group are aware of this or not. Historical consciousness, considered as a mode of consciousness different from though continuous with scientific, philosophical, poetic, religious, and mythic consciousness (to use Cassirer's classification of the modes of consciousness), is characterized by the predominance of the categories of modality for the representation and analysis of reality apprehended as being "historical" in its nature. It is the degree of awareness of the predominance of the categories of modality — and the prominence given to the elaboration of this awareness in reflections on history — that distinguishes "normal historians" from their openly theoretical (always *too* theoretical) enemies, "philosophers of history," as they are called (always disparagingly). Normal historiography is based on the dream of a theory-less knowledge — which would mean a "blind" knowledge insofar as by the term "theory" we might mean something like what the Greek term meant, i.e., "sight," "prospectus," etc.

That philosophy of history — a historical consciousness conscious of the necessity of a theory of its own practice — is continuous with, rather than antithetical to normal history is confirmed by the extent to which the former characteristically features the categories of modality in its practice. Witness: Hegel's notion of history as a

spectacle of the development of the *modes* of human consciousness, Marx's notion of history as the development of "the modes of
production," Vico's notion of history as the development of *modes*
of (poetic) figuration, and Spengler's notion of history as a cycle of
modal transformations analogous to those met with in mathematics
and music alike — the modes of something like Nietzsche's "spirit of
music."

It is not that a historical perspective excludes consideration of
reality under the categories of quantity, quality, and relation. It is
only that the *historicity* of this reality is comprehensible primarily in
terms of the categories of *modality* (possibility-impossibility, existence-nonexistence, necessity-contingency). Whatever "history"
may be — in contrast to "nature," "spirit," or whatever else we may
conceive the ahistorical dimensions of reality to be — it is graspable
as history only insofar as it appears as a *system in process of change*,
which the notion of *modality* alone is capable of doing justice to in
a manner that is cognitively responsible to the data of history, on
the one side, and our awareness of the *limits* of our understanding
of these data, on the other. Whence the rectitude of the intuition
that an *ideological* representation of history is characterized always
by some assertion about the real, true or ultimate meaning of history, that it claims to have explained the whole historical process or
even some part of it exhaustively and in full detail, and to be able,
not only to explain everything worth explaining in the past, but also
to be able to explain the present fully and to predict the course that
human development *must* follow in any imaginable future. In the
realm of historical knowledge, ideology is marked by a fall from (or
suppression of) consciousness into quantitative, qualitative, or
relational thinking (as in positivism, idealism, and structuralism,
respectively). On this view, the counterideological force of Marx's
idea of history would consist not so much of its materialism or its
discovery that the ultimate determining instance of historical
causation resides in the modes of production and their relationship
to the social relations of production, etc., but on its insistence on
modality as the ultimate determining instance of a specifically historical comprehension of history. Which is what, as I would see it,

the term "dialectical" in the phrase "dialectical materialism" is all about. Counterideological criticism, then, a criticism capable of guarding against and providing an autocritique of the inherent and ineluctably "ideological" elements in its own constitution, would be a criticism which founds the historical (or historicist) moment in its practice, not on a specific philosophy or theory of the true nature of historical events, a theory of historical causation, or some notion of history as an epiphenomenon of some other order of being (such as nature or spirit), but rather on a "view" of history as a system undergoing constant changes in both its forms and its contents, on the one side, and in the *modes* in which the forms and the contents are related to one another, on the other side.

This is why a "theory of modes" is a necessary (though not a sufficient) precondition of a distinctively historical perspective on reality. And this is why a specifically "historical criticism," a critical practice informed by a specifically historical consciousness of its object of study's "historicity," must presuppose or entail a "theory of modes" as a necessary precondition of its practice. And it is for reasons such as these that we might be able to account for Frye's placement of the topic of "historical criticism" as the first of the four kinds of critical practices he chose to examine in his *Anatomy.* This placement signals the intention to produce a metatheory of literary criticism that will be scientific, which is to say, counterideological; and counterideological precisely in the degree to which it takes historical consciousness as the *proteros* or first note, the note that sets the tone, for the consideration of the other *modes* of criticism identified by him as requiring individual characterization and analysis. Considered as a reflection on various *modes* of critical practice, each of which bears a *modal* relationship to all the others, the "First Essay," on "Historical Criticism: Theory of Modes," provides the basis for a specifically *historical* reflection on relations among these critical practices, including that of a distinctively "historical criticism." And this privileging of historical reflection negates the charges of formalism, mere structuralism, and ahistoricism often leveled by Left theorists of criticism against the *Anatomy.* The *Anatomy* is not *formalist* in its primary orientation but rather *modalist,* and as such is more historicist, less ideological, than the perspective provided by those theorists who claim to be able to see through the "forms" of history and to have grasped its true "contents" without ever having reflected at all on the problem of the "form-content" distinction itself.

What gets *repeated* in (literary) history is "mode" (not myth, not symbol, not even genre). An age or period will appear to repeat an earlier one because it shares a common *mode* (e.g., the repetition of "classical" forms and contents in the fifteenth- and sixteenth-century Renaissance).

Frye's critics have seized upon his theory of myths as the substance of his theory of history or, in the case of Jameson, his theory of symbols. But every new period of cultural (no less than of social) history is marked by a modal transformation which, because mode has to do with ratios of relationships (rather than with forms or contents), cannot but resemble in some way the mode of some period preceding it. Thus, if there is such a thing as postmodernism, it will resemble *in mode* some period other than that of modernism itself—even though its informing myths, privileged symbols, and dominant generic conventions may very well be those associated with the modernism to which it bears the historical (modal) relationship signified by the prefix "post" (*meta* or "coming after"). Thus, for example, the putative referentiality, narrativity, pastiche aspect, spatialization, etc., of postmodernism *resembles* the "realism" against which modernism reacted, but more in *mode* than in "myth," "symbol," or "genre."

What about the kinds of modes adumbrated by Frye in the "First Essay": the two genera (fictional and thematic) and the species thereof: mythic, romantic, high-mimetic, low-mimetic, and ironic, indicated as common to both genera of modes; the registers ("naive" and "sentimental"); and the ratios of relationship ascribed to them (their status as "phases" in a recurring but constantly evolving cycle of occurrences)? It is obvious that the modes identified as characterizing the fictional (forms) and thematic (contents) of literary works direct attention to the categories that permit reflection on sociospatial relationships: superior-equal-inferior (relationships figurated by the relations of the protagonist to his milieux in the modalities of fiction), and centered, marginalized, and excluded (relationships figured by the relations of the poet to his audience in the modalities of theme). Here "scale" would correspond to measures of *degree*, and "tone" would correspond to measures of *kind* that mark the distinctive modes by which similarity and difference are apprehended in a given instance of *stylized* (or fashioned) utterance. The notion of mode functions, exactly as it does in the thought of Hegel, Marx, Vico, Spengler, and so on, namely, as marking the specific structures of subordination and domination within any given disposition of the "means" of historical production and reproduction. Interestingly enough, the categories used by Frye for characterizing the fictional and thematic modes of literary production (and of cultural production in general) are explicitly *social* and *economic* (in the extended meaning of the latter term, i.e., "house management" or "management of expenditure") in nature. The relationships presumed to exist between a protagonist and his milieux, on the one side, and between the poet and his audience, on the other, presuppose distinctive modalities for construing the relationships obtaining among the "means" of literary (and by extension, cultural and social) production and reproduction. The dialectical relationship between the processes of production *and* reproduction, Frye grasps in the figure of "repetition" conceived, in the manner of Kierkegaard but in a way conformable to the thought of Hegel, Marx, Vico, and Spengler, i.e., as *modal* transformation. Change the means and you change the mode; change the mode and you affect the relationships obtaining among the means. In either case, what you end up with is a distinctively *historical* kind of change: which is to say, a difference in similarity or the reverse, a changing continuum or a continuity in change.

It is because Frye has grasped that historical process, unlike natural process grasped at the gross or supraatomic level of organic organization, is characterized preeminently by modal relationships and their transformations, rather than by discontinuous or catastrophic changes in either the forms or the contents of social and cultural phenomena, that his work seems so formalist to critics still indentured to a nineteenth-century "realist" view of history and its processes. The fundamental, or modal presupposition of this "realist" view is that of "viewing" itself. Realistic history favors the illusion that history— whether conceived as "the past" or as a process of change by which past, present, and future are linked together in a unitary temporal continuum—can be comprehended in the manner of a "seeing," as if it were accessible to "visual" perception. But neither the past, nor for that matter, the present, much less the future, nor the process of which these are considered to be phases or periods, can be "seen." If they could be so apprehended, it would be possible to represent them adequately in pictures or other kinds of visual images. That we might wish to believe that history could be apprehended as though "seen" is perfectly understandable, given the fact that, in our culture, "sight" is the sense we privilege as the principal arbiter between truth and falsity, the real and the illusory. History—the past or the process— would yield its secret could we but "see" it: seeing is believing.

But the problematic of historical inquiry (that *historia* inaugurated by Herodotus) is laid down by the realization that the past is inhabited by all those things which were once "seeable" but *are no longer so.* Or if we take history to be a process rather than a (temporal) place, "the past," the problematic motivating our inquiry is laid down by the circumstance that it is a process that can only be apprehended by its effects on a system and grasped as a concept that can be posited by thought or imagination, but never directly perceived.

The dynamics of historical inquiry, representation, and analysis arise from the disparity between our desire for some equivalent of a visual perception of objects and processes that are apprehendable only by traces of the "sounds" they once emitted (cf. "Ozymandias"), only in the extent to which they "speak" to us or can be made to respond to our verbal interrogations of them. As Jameson says, "History is not a text, but we have access to it only by way of its prior textualizations." Material remains of "the past," which, by their "ruination" (and resistance to it), *show* the effects of history as process, can be made into distinctively historical evidence only in the extent to which these remains can be made to speak, transformed into or endowed with "texts" that can be "read" as if "heard." As Jameson says, "History can be apprehended only through its effects, and never directly as some reified force" (102). This is why a distinctively historical knowledge of history is a knowledge based primarily on the assessment of evidence that is more *aural* than visual in nature. The peculiar problematic of historical knowledge is laid down by the circumstance that we know "the past" only by its "words," and the "historical process" only by its effects. This means that we "hear" and "feel" history rather than see it.

Jacques Barzun recently remarked that history can never be "taught," it can only be "read." Frye remarks relevantly:

> The world of social action and event, the world of time and process, has a particularly close association with the ear. The ear listens, and the ear translates what it hears into practical conduct. The world of individual thought and idea has a correspondingly close association with the eye, and nearly all our expressions for thought, from the Greek *theoria* down, are connected with visual metaphors. (243)

What might a comment such as this tell us of "Historical Criticism: Theory of Modes"?

Well, for one thing it tells us that "theory" of modes is a product of an effort to translate what is essentially an "aural" apprehension into something like a "visual" equivalent. Second, it suggests that "historical" criticism must begin with the effort to "hear" as much "how" the evidence "sounds" as "what" it "says." Third, it suggests that a historical knowledge of literature will consist of the comprehension of the relation between the "how" of "saying" and the "what" of saying: i.e., the *modal* relations obtaining between the fictional and the thematic modes of literary artifacts. In the translation of this "hearing" into a "seeing," there will be some slippage, some loss of meaning. But if hearing and seeing are themselves viewed, less as either forms or contents of perception, than, rather, as *modes*, this translation will be at once more "certain" and more "true" than any translation based upon a simplistic notion of the history of literature considered as either a succession of forms or a succession of contents could ever be.

Works Cited

Frye, Northrop. *Anatomy of Criticism: Four Essays.* Princeton: Princeton UP, 1957.

Jameson, Fredric. *The Political Unconscious: Narrative as a Socially Symbolic Act.* Ithaca: Cornell UP, 1981.

What's a Meta Phor?

Patricia Parker

In choosing for my title the *jeu de mots* of another Canadian, Marshall McLuhan—"A man's reach must exceed his grasp or what's a meta for?"—I wanted the emphasis in my return to Frye's conception of metaphor in the *Anatomy of Criticism* to fall both on "meta" (including the metacommentary it offers and has been identified with) and on "phor," in order to preserve the Greek root of bearing or transport conveyed in the famous *epiphora* of Aristotle's definition of metaphor which the *Anatomy* both recalls and transforms. But for a terrible moment and with a bizarre cybernetic twist that McLuhan, as well as the Frye who once humorously described himself as an unpredictable word processor (*Great Code* x), might recognize, I was told that the programming for the titles to be printed up in the brochure for the program on Frye I was to address might not take "Phor" as a separate lexical item, whatever the paronomastic point to be made.

I want to begin, however, not immediately with this "meta" or with the conception of metaphor outlined in *Anatomy of Criticism* but with two anecdotes, one of which will lead into the substance of a juxtaposition between the *Anatomy*'s foundational concept of metaphorical "identity" and developments in subsequent literary theory, most notably the work of Paul de Man. The first comes from an experience I had soon after I had joined the faculty of Victoria College and was speaking with Frye about de Man over lunch at the Vic High Table. To my surprise—and in a way that will take us directly into a lesser-known genesis of the *Anatomy*—Frye remarked that one of the several things that connected his work with de Man's was the powerful influence on both of them of the poetics of Mallarmé. It surprised me at the time to hear Frye say how important Mallarmé had been to him, though I had known from my own work on French symbolist poetry of his 1952 essay in *Yale French Studies* ("Three Meanings of Symbolism"), which is cited in *Anatomy* as providing much of the background and substance of its Second Essay. The importance of Mallarmé to both Frye and de Man is something I want to turn to first as a way of viewing the description of metaphorical identity in that Second Essay in contrast to the wariness of precisely such "identity" not just in the work of de Man, but in the poetry of another modern poet important for Frye—Wallace Stevens.

The other, earlier anecdote also involves Frye and de Man in relation to metaphor. The concentrated discussion of "levels" of metaphor at the conclusion of the Second Essay of *Anatomy of Criticism* ends with "anagogic" metaphor ("A *is* B") as distinct from conceptions of metaphor which see it as a shortened form of simile ("A is like B") or analogy ("A is to B as X is to Y") and so on. It is this more "radical" conception, as he calls it there, that becomes Frye's working definition of metaphor in the writing which comes out of the *Anatomy* in the decades that followed it. In the *Anatomy* itself, Frye's example of this "hypothetical" identity (and "hypothetical" is the crucial term to which we will return) is not a spatial but rather a temporal example of something illustrating "the process of identifying two independent forms": "A grown man feels identical with himself at age of seven, although the two manifestations of this identity, the man and the boy, have very little in common as regards similarity or likeness" (*Anatomy* 124). The form in which this example of copular or anagogic metaphor was presented in Frye's classroom lectures on the principles of the *Anatomy* to those of us enrolled in his graduate course in Literary Symbolism at Toronto in 1967 was as follows: "A person looking at a photograph of himself at age 7 would say, 'That's me' (or, if the student happened to be in Honors English, 'That is I')."

Several years later, when along with many others in an equally crowded room, I was a doctoral student in de Man's Yale seminar devoted to what he called the "aberrant" or "mad" identities of metaphor and its conflation of temporally separate episodes in Wordsworth's *Prelude*, I found myself, like so many others, both uncertain what he was getting at and, in graduate student fashion, desperate to say something, anything, to redeem myself. Because so much of what I was hearing sounded strangely familiar, I raised my hand and asked, "Professor de Man, when you speak of madness and aberrance, here, do you mean something like, say, just to take an example, someone looking at a photograph of himself at age seven and saying 'That's me' (or more properly, 'That is I')?" And he responded, just as the seminar was about to end, "Yes, that's it!"

I

I begin with these anecdotes because I want to focus on two questions—the relation of Mallarmé to the conception of "anagogic" metaphor in *Anatomy of Criticism*, and the connection as well as the divergence between Frye and de Man on the copular "identity" of metaphor, as a way of approaching the *meta* of metaphor in the *Anatomy* from the thirty-year perspective of its place in contemporary criticism.

In the early *Yale French Studies* essay on Symbolism and Mallarmé in which he articulates the principles of centrifugal and centripetal reading that would be central to the *Anatomy* five years later, Frye distinguishes *symbolisme*—"mainly French-inspired, Catholic and intensely conservative"—from what he calls the mythopoeic and "archetypal" poetry running from Spenser through Milton, to Blake, Shelley, and Keats, which he characterizes as "mainly English-inspired, Protestant and revolutionary" ("Three Meanings" 16-17). It is in the context of this contrast that Frye develops in this early essay the conception of "the symbol as archetype or myth" that would be central to the Second Essay of the *Anatomy*. And the essay's ending—on the paucity of critical attention to the great English mythopoeic poets as opposed to the Symbolist poetry favored by a New Criticism less receptive to that more radical English tradition—is, on rereading from the perspective of the explosion in criticism the *Anatomy* itself inspired, a rare historical glimpse into the awesome influence Frye's work was to have on the establishment of a canon now so secure as to make it impossible to believe that these poets, in 1952, were relatively ignored.

But it is this early essay's description of Symbolism—which Frye cites as "largely paraphrased from Mallarmé"—that I want to focus on for a moment, as a way of exploring how the same poet led to such divergent directions in the work of Frye and de Man. The paraphrase from Mallarmé which stands at its center needs to be cited in full:

> Poetry leads us from the material thing though the verbal symbol as sign, into the verbal symbol as image, and thence into an apprehension of the Word, the unity of poetic experience. It follows that the relation of the material thing to the spiritual mystery of the Word is a kind of sacramental relation. Thus *symbolisme*, like the Courtly Love convention before it, resolves into an elaborate analogy of religion. The poet's attitude to his public is not democratic but catholic. He should avoid anything like rhetoric, or the marketplace view of words as like coins, to be exchanged, not for their own sakes, but as a medium for actions toward things. So far from being introspective or solipsistic, however, the poet as a personality is not in his poem at all. He is a priest of a mystery; he turns his back on his hearers, and invokes, chanting in a hieratic tongue, the real presence of the Word which reveals the mystery. It is only within that Presence that he and his hearers communicate, and the experience is always new, for the Word is of a virgin birth. (14)

Apart from the question of the relation of Frye's paraphrase, in 1952, to the Mallarméan prose texts from which it draws, this description of the hieratic function of the poet of *symbolisme* most closely recalls one particular Mallarméan poem. Because it is one which also depends crucially on the root of "phor" with which we began—and hence complexly summons up the *epiphora* or "phor" of metaphor—it might be worth pausing over it in order to approach the divergences in modern criticism and theory in which a view of metaphor holds such a crucial place.[1] The poem, which must be cited in French, is the so-called "Sonnet en x," because of its striking initial rhyme:

> Ses purs ongles très haut dédiant leur onyx,
> L'Angoisse, ce minuit, soutient, lampadophore,

Maint rêve vespéral brûlé par le Phénix
Que ne recueille pas de cinéraire amphore

Sur les crédences, au salon vide: nul ptyx,
Aboli bibelot d'inanité sonore.
(Car le Maître est allé puiser des pleurs au Styx
Avec ce seul objet dont le Néant s'honore).

Mais proche la croiseé au nord vacante, un or
Agonise selon peut-être le décor
Des licornes ruant du feu contre une nixe,

Elle, défunte nue en le miroir, encor
Que, dans l'oubli fermé par le cadre, se fixe
De scintillations sitôt le septuor.

This enigmatic Mallarméan sonnet begins with a hieratic gesture,
reminiscent of the Mass and the religious hierophant ("Ses purs
ongles trés haut dédiant"). Its language summons up the ritual of
the Mass (even more specifically the midnight Mass before an
Easter resurrection or apocalyptic dawn) and the "croisée" of the
Cross, along with other terms suggestive of a whole hieratic context, including, in "Maître," a host absent or dead reminiscent of
the Christian "Seigneur." The Ovidian metamorphosis of the final
lines of this sonnet "en x" (the nymph Callisto, violated by Zeus,
transformed first into a bear and then translated into the heavens
as *Ursa Major* or "le Septuor") is joined by the Eucharistic sugges-
tion of the elevated host in the opening dedicatory gesture
("dédiant") and thus by the "X" of the definitive *mythos* of translation, the master-mystery of a coupling of divine and human (the
deus-homo who "is" both God and Man) that guarantees not only
the mediatory efficacy of the Mass itself, but also the "credence" of
words in the Word, a "translation" of which the Cross of Christ as
"phénix" is traditionally the vehicle. The syntactic possibility that it
is "L'Angoisse, ce minuit," which is "lamp-bearing" or "lampadophore," recalls the tripartite liturgical structure associated
precisely with the "x" or Cross—death, disappearance, and
resurrection or return—and in particular its middle or transitional
stage, the mourned absence of the Master whose descent to the

Styx was the prelude to a resurrection. Within this tradition, the corresponding temporal image is the movement from midnight ("ce minuit") to dawn and the theological metaphorization of moon and stars as faithful "lamp-bearers" from the sacrificed sun ("un or agonise") to a apocalyptic dawn or Light, "X" as the apocalyptic sign of the return of the true Morning Star (Matthew 24:27), the end of mediation and of metaphor.[2]

The most obvious, and most frequently commented on, feature of this enigmatic Mallarméan sonnet is its Greek-sounding rhymes not just in "x" but in "phor(e)." And it is the latter — in a sonnet described by Mallarmé as "allegorical of itself . . . reflecting itself in every way" (*Oeuvres* 1488-90) — that summons up the sense of transfer, transport, or bearing at the root of the Aristotelian *epiphora*, of metaphor as *translatio*, translation, or figure of "transport."[3] The sonnet contains a whole group of terms from the traditional lexicon of the "translation" effected by the "Word," including the "light-bearing" ("lampadophore") of that "X" who figures in the section of the *Anatomy* devoted to "apocalyptic" metaphor. But the poem can also be read, in its very foregrounding of this language, as undercutting or subverting the entire tradition of this hieratic gesture and the telos of this metaphorical light-bearing. Dawn ("aurore"), in a sonnet which contains within it both "vespéral" and "minuit," is a rhyme-word conspicuous by its absence in a series of rhymes that might only too readily make use of it. The poem might even be seen as marking a signal moment — the moment of *symbolisme* — which severs the connection with the anagogic, the teleological, and the apocalyptic destination of metaphor itself.

The traditional metaphor of conversion (the death which "*is*" life) recalls the structure of what Paul Ricoeur calls "la métaphore vive" (*La Métaphore*), an apparent death on one level which turns out to be life on another. But Mallarmé's sonnet does not allow us to say for certain whether something is alive or dead ("Que ne recueille pas de cinéraire amphore / Sur les crédences, au salon vide: nul ptyx"; the "Styx" in line 7 is not clearly crossed). The promise in "X" or the Christian "Seigneur," of a definitive resurrection and translation is undercut in the poem by the Janus-like or two-faced aspect of phrases which make impossible a reading in any single direction. "Lampadophore" itself might just as readily be translated as a Greek, or Greekified, version of the Latin "Lucifer" ("light-bearing"), not just the planet Venus reappearing as the Morning Star after its disappearance as Vesper ("Maint rêve vespéral") but also Satan as fallen "Star of the Morning" (Isaiah 14:12), the master of imposture who resembles Christ as the true "lampadophore" or "Morning Star" (Revelation 22:5) and whose vestments bear the "onyx" of the true hierophant (Exodus 28:9; Ezekiel 28:13), a combination of resemblance and bearing which makes Lucifer a potential figure for metaphor itself.

The possibility of an illusory of "Luciferic" bearing thus joins the double face of an opening whose "ongles" and gesture suggest a sinister Mass as much as a Christian one and the reminder (in "licornes ruant du feu contre une nixe") that the story of the unicorn caught by a virgin—a figure for the mysterious joining of the two natures in Christ—is a story of treachery, of trust in a virgin who could appropriately be termed "une nixe" ("une x").

There is no assurance that the light-bearing of "lampadophore" leads at all to a dawn, of whether the "un or / Agonise" of the sestet, with its generic expectation of the usual sonnet turn ("Mals") is a sun struggling to be born or the death agony of the "vesperal" one—or indeed whether all such metaphoric translations, the promise of resurrection tied to a solar return, can be anything more than metaphor.

Roger Dragonetti has situated Mallarmé's poetics within the disappearance of any "Maître" or transcendental "Word," signalling what he calls in Mallarmé the "abolished dawn" of "le Verbe."[4] With all of its figures of *translatio* or crossing, and all its summoning of the lexicon of theological transport, there is in this poem no definite arrival, no final destination for what is being carried across. "Lampadophore" itself is suspended, capable of several references or of none. What is foregrounded would seem to be the activity of bearing, or translation, itself, *metapherein* in its root (Greek) sense. And the reader might well ask what "credence" would be appropri-

ate for something which simply "bears," for which there is no counterpart of "les crédences," no definitive *credenza* or test of the difference between a true "light-bearing" and an illusory, or Luciferic,
one.

I touch on this particular poem of Mallarmé as a bridge between
Frye and de Man in part because this "luciferic" lightbearing reap-
pears in a signal essay of de Man's on the positional power and status of metaphor. I quote from the conclusion of the essay on
Shelley's *Triumph of Life*, written for *Deconstruction and Criticism*
and since collected in *The Rhetoric of Romanticism*:

> The repetitive erasures by which language performs the erasure of its own
> positions can be called disfiguration. The disfiguration of Rousseau is
> enacted in the text, in the scene of the root, and repeats itself in a more gen-
> eral mode in the disfiguration of the shape:
>
>> . . . The fair shape waned in the coming light
>> As veil by veil the silent splendour drops
>> From Lucifer amid the chrysolite
>> Of sunrise ere it strike the mountain tops — (*Rhetoric* 119)

"Lucifer, or metaphor," as de Man glosses these lines, "the bearer
of light which carries over the light of the senses and of cognition
from events and entities to their meaning, irrevocably loses the
contour of its own face or shape" (*Rhetoric* 119). And the essay
traces, through *The Triumph of Life*, both metaphor as the arbitrary positing power of language and the impossibility of calling a
halt to its ceaseless movement. The seduction of the figure, in de
Man's reading of Shelley here, is that "it creates an *illusion*" of
meaning (120, my emphasis). In Shelley's poem, Adam's explana-
tion to Eve in Milton's *Paradise Lost* of the teleological and mediatory function of light-bearing, of the lesser lights which lead to the
Star of the Morning and the greater light of a final, apocalyptic
dawn, is transformed into a ceaseless motion of positing and effac-
ing, a process which (in contrast to the Miltonic anagogy or telos) is
"endless," resistant, as de Man puts it, to any "monumentalizing,"
sytematizing, or fixing (120).

De Man is much more wary of the copular "identity" of metaphor than is Frye, whose working definition of metaphor in the writing which followed the *Anatomy of Criticism* is the very "A is B" that forms the "error" or aberrance with which so much of de Man's writing is concerned, from the "seductions" of the figure in *Blindness and Insight* to the identification of the "dancer" with the "dance" in the lead essay of *Allegories of Reading.* Indeed, in a reading of the *Anatomy* as the kind of metacommentary that would be precisely the opposite of this Shelleyan movement in its monumentalizing, it is Frye's celebration of metaphorical identity which might stand out as farthest from de Man's post-Nietzschean sense of the error of "identifying what cannot be identified" (*Allegories* 11). It is, however, perhaps best through juxtaposition with yet another poet important for Frye — Wallace Stevens — that some of the dimensions of the problem of "identity" and its relation to the *Anatomy's* foundational concept of metaphor might best be explored.

II

Stevens figures only in a footnote to the *Anatomy*, but is the subject of an essay published in *The Hudson Review* in the very same year (eventually incorporated into *Fables of Identity*) which makes it clear how comprehensive a familiarity he had with the work of this poet even while forging the notions of metaphor central to the *Anatomy* as a whole. Stevens is still a presence in Frye's thinking as late as *The Great Code*, including the conclusion to "Metaphor II," the chapter which presents in more elaborated form the copular metaphor of the Christ who "is" God and man which yields the tables of apocalyptic and demonic imagery in the *Anatomy* itself. Stevens is also the poet of "The Motive for Metaphor," which provided the title of the first section of Frye's *The Educated Imagination* of 1963, the series of CBC radio talks which were a kind of *Anatomy of Criticism* for the Canadian general public and which, as a teaching text in schools, have been the form in which generations of Canadian students have first encountered the *Anatomy's* principles. It is that informal text of radio lectures which describes "the loss and regaining of identity" as the "framework of all literature" and which ends its opening discussion with the capturing in the imagination of "that original lost sense of identity with our surroundings, where there is nothing outside the mind of man, or something identical with the mind of man" (*Educated* 55, 29). Stevens' poem is cited in full at the end of the chapter to which it lends its name:

> You like it under the trees in autumn,
> Because everything is half dead.
> The wind moves like a cripple among the leaves
> And repeats words without meaning.
>
> In the same way, you were happy in spring,
> With the half colors of quarter-things,
> The slightly brighter sky, the melting clouds,
> The single bird, the obscure moon —
>
> The obscure moon lighting an obscure world
> Of things that would never be quite expressed,
> Where you yourself were never quite yourself
> And did not want nor have to be,
>
> Desiring the exhilarations of changes:
> The motive for metaphor, shrinking from
> The weight of primary noon,
> The A B C of being,
>
> The ruddy temper, the hammer
> Of red and blue, the hard sound —
> Steel against intimation — the sharp flash,
> The vital, arrogant, fatal, dominant X.

"What Stevens calls the weight of primary noon," writes Frye — in one of the possible readings of this poem's syntactically ambiguous final lines — is "the A B C of being." The "dominant X" is "the objective world, the world set over against us"; and the evasions of metaphor, to use a familiar Stevensian locution, involve a turning from that "objective world" to something else (31). But when Frye describes this turning, he describes it in terms of a copular, or "anagogic" metaphorics:

As for metaphor, where you're really saying "this is that," you're turning your back on logic and reason completely, because logically two things can never be the same thing and still remain two things. The poet, however, uses these two crude, primitive, archaic forms of thought in the most uninhibited way, because his job is not to describe nature, but to show you a world completely absorbed and possessed by the human mind. (*Educated* 32-33)

This description of metaphor, informed by the ecstatic union of Shakespeare's "The Phoenix and the Turtle," used in the *Anatomy* as a principal instance of metaphoric identity, as by the great speech on "the lunatic, the lover and the poet" from *A Midsummer Night's Dream*, is, however, one whose copular Stevens might be slightly more wary of, as he might well be of the notion of "a world completely absorbed and possessed by the human mind." Indeed, Stevens' "Motive for Metaphor," in its opening description and its marked evasions of identity ("Where you yourself were never quite yourself / And did not want nor have to be, / Desiring the exhilarations of changes") might shrink from the "dominant X" of such an identifying and potentially "dominant" metaphor as much as from the fixed and unimaginative world of things as they are. For there is, in this "Motive," not only a subtle Shelleyan echoing in the "wind" of the poem's opening lines but a Shelleyan sense throughout of the movement (motive/*motus*) of metaphor.

Frye rightly notes, in the study of Stevens contemporaneous with *Anatomy of Criticism*, that in Stevens he has a poet whose concern with metaphor is as central to his poetic vocation as it is to his own critical one. Stevens' use of the term begins with his early work; and the variations on metaphor throughout both his poetry and his prose sound like a compendium history of its shifting conceptions, just as his meditations on Evening Star and Morning Star sound like a summa of twentieth-century philosophical discussions of the problem of "identity." But it is interesting that Frye should continue to cite Stevens—a poet wary of what he calls "anagogic" metaphor—from the time of an essay written in the same period as the *Anatomy*, though Stevens appears only marginally in a footnote within it, to the culminating discussion of the apocalyptic "identity" of metaphor which links the *Anatomy* to *The Great Code* across a

quarter century of criticism. For it is perhaps Stevens above all —
and the complexities of Frye's engagement with Stevens — that
would unfix the magisterial "meta" and the sense of fixity and
monumentality that Frye's "archetypal criticism" and the *Anatomy*
in particular have become identified with.

Let us begin with the discussion of this figure in Stevens in Frye's
1957 essay. "The normal unit of poetic expression is the
metaphor," writes Frye in that essay, "and Stevens was well aware
of the importance of metaphor, as is evident from the many poems
which use the word in title or text" (*Fables* 247). But his
"conception of metaphor is regrettably unclear"; and Frye goes on
both to chart those variations and to correct that lack of clarity. In
Stevens

> we often find metaphor used pejoratively in the poems as a form of avoiding
> direct contact with reality. The motive for metaphor, we are told, is the
> shrinking from immediate experience. Stevens appears to mean by such
> metaphor, however, simile or comparison, "the intricate evasions of as." And
> metaphor is actually nothing of the kind. In its literal grammatical form
> metaphor is statement of identity: this is that, A is B. (*Fables* 248; paren-
> thetical page references omitted)

Frye is very aware here of the necessity of differentiating what he
means by "a world of total metaphor, where everything is identified
as itself and with everything else," a "world where subject and
object, reality and mental organization of reality, are one" from the
"false unity of the dominating mind" or the "logical unity of the
generalizing reason," which destroys individuality and difference
(249). But we can also see in this essay the pressure of the conception of radical or anagogic metaphor from the *Anatomy* seeking to
correct the more pejorative senses of metaphor in Stevens:

> To sum up: the imaginative act breaks down the separation between subject
> and object, the perceiver shut up in "the enclosures of hypothesis" like an
> embryo in a "naked egg" or glass shell, and a perceived world similarly
> imprisoned in the remoteness of its "irreducible X," which is also an egg.
> Separation is then replaced by the direct, primitive identification which
> Stevens ought to have called metaphor and which, not having a word for it,
> he calls "description" in one of his definitive poems, a term to which he else-
> where adds "apotheosis" and "transformation," which come nearer to what

he really means. . . . The theoretical postulate of Stevens' poetry is a world of total metaphor, where the poet's vision may be identified with anything it visualizes. For such poetry the most accurate word is apocalyptic, a poetry of "revelation" in which all objects and experiences are united with a total mind, Such poetry gives us:

> . . . the book of reconciliation,
> Book of a concept only possible
> In description, canon central in itself,
> The thesis of the plentifullest John.
>   (*Fables* 251-52)[5]

Stevens, in his sense of "description," however, and in the more evasive of his motives for metaphor, is much more wary than Frye both of the identifications of the copula and of this "revelation." Frye goes on from this citation in 1957 to speak of "apocalypse," in his special sense of the term as "a world of total metaphor." But Stevens, as one of his most canny (and Frye-influenced) recent readers points out, is more "eucalyptic" than apocalyptic (Cook, "Directions"),[6] and it is to her subtle dialogue between Stevens and Frye that we might, in viewing the "meta" of metaphor in the legacy of the *Anatomy*, most usefully turn.

III

As Eleanor Cook points out in her magisterial recent study of the poetry of Stevens, Stevens is much more wary of anagogic metaphor than Frye, at least until late in his life (*Poetry, Word-Play* 175-76). She begins this study with the early Stevens poem from *Harmonium* entitled "Metaphors of a Magnifico," which Helen Vendler reads as a problem in psychological identity but which she reads as a problem of archetypal as against other types of metaphor, and so therefore also as "a problem of both identity and totality" (176-77). The "magnifico" of the poem's title "keeps trying to get his men across a bridge, like some officer in charge of transport." But if this is a "bridge of metaphor"—as Stevens' later play on "transport" in relation to metaphor in *Transport to Summer* seems to suggest—the movement never seems to get "across" or "at least never past archetypal metaphor, which seems to get nowhere" (177). "The poem centers its five symmetrical stanzas on the one-word line that is the bridge of all metaphor, the verb 'to be'," (177) and begins:

> Twenty men crossing a bridge,
> Into a village,
> Are twenty men crossing twenty bridges,
> Into twenty villages,
> Or one man
> Crossing a single bridge into a village.

But its copular "are" only, as Cook remarks, "carries A back to A, and no meta—, no 'beyond' comes" (177). The "magnifico's problem seems to be archetypal metaphor," which "goes dead and seems inimical to the language of sensuous particulars. Stevens is drawn to particulars, yet something in him also wants archetypal metaphor, as we realize from his hero and major-man figures" (177-78). As Cook brilliantly reads this poem—and Stevens on metaphor in a subtle, sotto voce dialogue with Frye—this "magnifico" offers us

> Stevens testing his own "magnifying" poetic self against his sensuous, partic-
> ular, poetic self. In *Sunday Morning*, m-sounds say "mmm" to "magnificent"
> Jove and his mythy mind. "Mmm" may express pleasure or express skepti-
> cism—a fine double sense for *Sunday Morning* and for the "magnifico"
> among Stevens' own selves. (178)

Cook notes how many of Stevens' poems play with the copular— such as "God Is Good. It Is a Beautiful Night," or "Oak Leaves Are Hands"—and notes in the latter case that Stevens, more "Manichean" than Frye, even leaves open the possibility of copular metaphor daemonized and gone awry (173-74, 179-80). I would add to this that the subtle Stevensian variations on the copula—on the status of the "is" in "A is B"—include as well the frequent impossibility of distinguishing (at least in grammatical form) between what Frye calls "the logical unity of the generalizing reason"—whose copulas take the form of statements (including the kind of statement subtly reproduced, analyzed, and parodied in

Stevens' own poetry of statement)—and the copular identity or "this is that" of the imagination.[7]

The "is" of the "A is B" that produces the metaphor of identity—"a world completely absorbed and possessed by the human mind" or "that original lost sense of identity with our surroundings, where there is nothing outside the mind of man, or something identical with the mind of man," as *The Educated Imagination* puts it (33, 29)—may equally produce that imperializing and monumentalizing identity or synthesis from which the ambiguous "you" of "The Motive for Metaphor" might be said to "shrink." Stevens maintains a more cautious sense of the nearness of a "hypothetical" identity (Frye) to an aberrant one (de Man), as in the "chord that falsifies" of a chilling section of "The Man with the Blue Guitar" XI):

Slowly the ivy on the stones
Becomes the stones. Women become

The cities, children become the fields
And men in waves become the sea,

It is the chord that falsifies.
The sea returns upon the men,

The fields entrap the children, brick
Is a weed and all the flies are caught.

In pursuit of the problem of identity—and of the lookalikes of grammatical statement and metaphorical copula—if we were to follow through what Frye in the essay on Stevens calls "the logical unity of the generalizing reason" or the "false unity of the dominating mind" (*Fables* 249) into the remarks on metaphor not in the Second Essay of the *Anatomy* but in the fascinating and still unmined conclusion to the Fourth Essay ("Rhetorical Criticism") on the relation of rhetoric to both grammar and logic, we might again be led back to a juxtaposition of de Man and Frye, though this time somewhat differently. What Frye outlined in 1957 as an imperative for future criticism ("the possibility of links between grammar and rhetoric, and between rhetoric and logic, that have a neglected but crucial importance" [*Anatomy* 334]) might be seen as initiated, precisely, in the analyses of the "grammatization of rhetoric" and the "rhetorization of grammar" that begin *Allegories of Reading*; and his suggestions that the "only road from grammar to logic . . . runs through the intermediary territory of rhetoric" (*Anatomy* 331) and that "literature may be described as the rhetorical organization of grammar and logic" (*Anatomy* 245), uncannily anticipate the complexities of the prospect that de Man delineates. It might even be said—to go back to the "aberrant" or "mad" identifications of metaphor in *The Prelude* with which we began—that if we were to historicize Frye's conception of "anagogic" metaphor against the history outlined by Foucault, as well as against the work of de Man, what Frye singles out in this concluding essay of the *Anatomy* as the long subordination of rhetoric to the "place of honor in Western culture" (337) accorded to the discursive reason—the same discursivity that treats metaphor or the "fallacies spawned by paronomasia" (332) as an aberrant and a dangerous fallacy—might take us as well to the whole history of enlightenment and postenlightment wariness of this aberrance and these identifications that marks the poetry of Wordsworth, the poetry of Stevens, and perhaps as well, complexly, the writing of de Man.

It is a history, as well, that the *Anatomy*, even with its insistence on anagogy, might not, finally, be able to stand outside. And so it is with a Stevens in dialogue with the *Anatomy*'s foundation in copular or anagogic metaphor that we might need to return to the "meta" of metaphor in Frye and the "metacommentary" the *Anatomy* is taken to provide. De Man, more than Frye, perhaps, is in tune with the post-Shelleyan and post-Nietzschean, or perhaps even Stevensian, wariness of the aberrant and potentially dangerous identifications of metaphor. Frye's privileging of identity—his continuing emphasis on and commitment to what unifies rather than what divides—gives an "apocalyptic" cast to all of his criticism. And the notion of metaphoric "identity" at the center of *Anatomy of Criticism* recurs again and again in the works that followed it, as in this passage at the end of the book on Milton entitled *The Return of Eden*:

> To use terms which are not Milton's but express something of his attitude, the central myth of mankind is the myth of lost identity: the goal of all reason, courage and vision is the regaining of identity. The recovery of identity is not the feeling that I am myself and not another, but the realization that there is only one man, one mind, and one world, and that all walls of partition have been broken down forever. (143)

"Walls of partition," here, comes from the anagogic or apocalyptic dimension of the passage in Ephesians 2 on the coming of Christ (or "X"), and there is perhaps no more resonant statement in all of Frye of the further apocalyptic reaches of metaphorical identity. Frye insists in this work, as he does in the passage on anagogic metaphor in *Anatomy of Criticism* or the 1957 essay on Stevens, that "total identity is not uniformity, still less monotony, but a unity of various things" (*Anatomy* 125). But such statements of identity in this "one man, one mind," like Stevens' Magnifico or Major Man, can also make some of us nervous of its very oneness, and anxious for, if not partitions, at least a recognition of the differences that might make, to take just one of many potential dissensions from such a dominating unity, those of us who are not men, as more recent readings of Milton are attempting to outline, more uneasy about identification with that "one," even if we realize that "one man," in Frye's use, is to be read with its implicit footnote from another New Testament text, that in this apocalypse, "there is neither male nor female."[8]

Part of this problem might be got at in Frye, finally, by contrasting the tendency to synchrony in this copular "is" with the dynamism and diachrony of the biblical type, crucial and coexistent within Frye's work from the beginning. Metaphor, Frye writes in the passage we have quoted from *The Educated Imagination*, is the instrument of anagogy or "return," a "language of identification" through which poetry tries to "lead our imaginations back" to the identity figured in the stories of a lost Golden Age, Eden, or Hesperides, a "motive for metaphor" which makes the "story of the loss and regaining of identity" the "framework of all literature"

(53). The Christ who "*is* both the one God and the one Man, the
Lamb of God, the tree of life," and so on (*Anatomy* 141), according
to the principles of biblical symbolism outlined in the *Anatomy* and
The Great Code, is the principal instance of the "world of total
metaphor" that underlies both. But even in *Paradise Regained*,
which is English poetry's most explicit treatment of this plot of
return, the "is" of metaphor involves the danger of an aberrant, lit-
eralizing, or premature identification, and metaphor's apocalyptic
"identity" is qualified by the diachronicity of the biblical type, and
its recognition of discontinuity and temporal difference. The Bible
presents us, in Frye's words, with "a series of repetitions of what is
spiritually the same event" (in Milton's poem, the Son "is" Moses,
David, Solomon, and Job), but only in the Apocalypse do contigu-
ity and succession drop away. Even the Book of Apocalypse, the
culture's definitive anagogic text, ends its vision of paradise
regained in the prospective mode of an "Even so, come."

Frye keeps insisting on the contingent and "hypothetical" nature
of metaphorical "identity." The whole discussion of it, indeed, in
the Second Essay of *Anatomy of Criticism*, begins with its statement
in a form much less potentially hypostatizing than the more frequent use he makes of the copular "is": "metaphor, in its radical
form, is a statement of identity of the 'A is B' type, or rather,
putting it into its proper hypothetical form, of the 'let X be Y'
type" (123). And the discussion ends with a passage on the inter-
play between poetry and religion which underscores the constant
need of the former to break down the latter's tendency to
"intellectual idolatry," the mistaking of a present formulation for a
final one, in a way that sounds much more like Stevens than the
stereotype of the *Anatomy* as synchronic and static might lead a
new generation of readers to believe. Stevens, in fact — and
specifically, the Stevens of the "imperfect" in the sense of the not-
yet-complete — appears at the point in the discussion of metaphor
in *The Great Code* where Frye moves from a statement of apocalyptic "identity" to the decentralization of "metaphors of unity and
integration" into something more discrete, into an "imperfect"
which is "not finished but continuously active" (168). The *OED*

reminds us that the Greek prefix "meta" is, strictly speaking, improperly used in the sense of the transcendent or "supra" — though it is this sense of it which gives to a certain reading of the metaperspective of the *Anatomy* the charge of a more monumentalizing synchrony. In a footnote to the discussion of metaphor in *The Great Code*, which returns to the "profoundly illogical, if not anti-logical" structure of the "A-is-B," Frye cites a more recent debt to the Ricoeur of *The Rule of Metaphor*, who is quick to point out that metaphor's "this is that" contains within it, always, an implicit undoing or "this is not." It is perhaps this "mental leap of metaphor," as the Fourth and final Essay of the *Anatomy* calls it — away from the "this is that" of descriptive statement or the translative certainty of discursive reason — that places Frye's conception of metaphor, finally, in the role of the "imperfect" in Stevens' sense as well. And it is perhaps this "meta" more properly used — something which moves "beyond" — that might describe the aspect of the *Anatomy* most in tune with the Shelleyan or Stevensian motion in the "motive for metaphor," and that gives to Frye's own work the more dynamic, and temporal, aspect of the "revolutionary" tradition he celebrated in that essay of 1952.

Notes

1 Metaphor is central not only to the work of Frye and de Man, of course, but also to the writing of Jacques Derrida, from "La mythologie blanche" forward. For an earlier treatment of Frye on metaphor, see my "Anagogic Metaphor."

2 For this traditional theological interpretation of waiting for an anagogic or apocalyptic "Day" when there will be no more need for lamp-bearing (the lamp of Revelation 22:5), see, for example, Aquinas, *Summa Theologiae* Ia.63.6 and 58.6-7, together with Augustine, *De genesi ad litteram* IV.22, 39 and XXX.47.

3 Puttenham in the Renaissance, for example, renders the Greek "metaphor" as the "Figure of Transport," and "translation" is routinely metaphor's early English name. I have dealt in more detail with the sense of "transport" that lies at the root of metaphor in "The Metaphorical Plot," in *Literary Fat Ladies*.

4 See Dragonetti, 208-209. The other reading of this sonnet that has been most useful in my own reading is Ellen Burt's "Mallarmé's 'Sonnet en *yx*.' "

5 The lines from Stevens are from "Description without Place." Frye's parenthetical page references are omitted.

6 "Eucalyptic" ("well-covered") as opposed to "apocalyptic" as uncovering comes from the "Professor Eucalyptus" of "An Ordinary Evening in New Haven."

7 Frye himself touches on this problem in a footnote to a sentence in the "Tentative Conclusion" to the *Anatomy* having to do with "discursive verbal structures": "The critic would of course need to distinguish an explicit metaphor from a metaphorical verbal construct. 'X has a bee in his bonnet about Y' is an explicit metaphor; 'X has got the notion Y into his head' is the verbal frame of the same metaphor, but for ordinary purposes it would pass as a simply descriptive statement" (364).

8 Galatians 3:38. The most subtle of the rereadings of Milton in this regard—a reading, again, engaged with the work of Frye—is the full-length study of Milton in relation both to apocalypse and to difference by Mary Nyquist, forth-

coming from Cornell University Press. Frye is consistently uncompromising, in his reading of the biblical tradition, about the gender identifications within it that are independent of biological gender—those which, for example, make all of Israel, male and female, symbolically female. In this respect, the complexities of his notion of "anagogic" metaphor—and of the "one man, one mind" so often cited as an example of the "world of pure metaphor"—in Frye generally might well be best approached through the similar complexities and culture-bound divisions in the work of Milton.

Works Cited

Burt, Ellen. "Mallarmé's 'Sonnet en *yx*': The Ambiguities of Speculation." *Yale French Studies* 54 (1977): 55-72.

Cook, Eleanor. "Directions in Reading Wallace Stevens: Up, Down, Across." *Lyric Poetry: Beyond New Criticism*. Ed. Chaviva Hosek and Patricia Parker. Ithaca: Cornell UP, 1985. 298-309

_____. *Poetry, Word-Play, and Word-War in Wallace Stevens*. Princeton: Princeton UP, 1988.

de Man, Paul. *Allegories of Reading*. New Haven: Yale UP, 1979.

_____. *Blindness and Insight: Essays in the Rhetoric of Contemporary Criticism*. Minneapolis: U of Minnesota P, 1983.

_____. *The Rhetoric of Romanticism*. New York: Columbia UP, 1984.

Derrida, Jacques. "La mythologie blanche." *Marges de la philosophie*. Paris: Editions de Minuit, 1972.

Dragonetti, Roger. *Lingue e Stile*. Bologna: Il Mulino, 1969.

_____. "Shelley Disfigured." *Deconstruction and Criticism*. Ed. Harold Bloom, et al. New York: Seabury, 1979. 39-73.

Frye, Northrop. *Anatomy of Criticism: Four Essays*. Princeton: Princeton UP, 1957.

_____. *The Educated Imagination.* Bloomington: Indiana UP, 1964.

_____. *Fables of Identity.* New York: Harcourt, 1963.

_____. *The Great Code: The Bible and Literature.* New York: Harcourt, 1982.

_____. *The Return of Eden: Five Essays on Milton's Epics.* Toronto: U of Toronto P, 1965.

_____. "Three Meanings of Symbolism." *Yale French Studies* 9 (1952): 11-19.

Mallarmé, Stéphane. *Oeuvres complétes.* Paris: Gallimard, 1945.

Parker, Patricia. "Anagogic Metaphor: Breaking Down the Walls of Partition." *Centre and Labyrinth: Essays in Honour of Northrop Frye.* Ed. Eleanor Cook, et al. Toronto: U of Toronto P, 1983. 38-58.

_____. *Literary Fat Ladies: Rhetoric, Gender, Property.* London: Methuen, 1987.

Ricoeur, Paul. *La Métaphore vive.* Paris: Editions du Seuil, 1976; trans. by Robert Czerny as *The Rule of Metaphor.* Toronto: U of Toronto P, 1977.

Ratio Contained by *Oratio*: Northrop Frye on the Rhetoric of Non-Literary Prose

Paul Hernadi

The last brief section of the Fourth Essay is among the least often cited segments of Northrop Frye's *Anatomy of Criticism*. This is surprising because the ideas rehearsed in the eleven pages entitled "The Rhetoric of Non-Literary Prose" (326-27) prefigure several current concerns in the study of texts. Foremost among these concerns is the question whether literature can be distinguished from nonliterature. In this paper I explore how Professor Frye, after considerable undisguised hesitation, winds up answering the question as many of us would answer it today: with a resolutely unequivocal "perhaps."

Frye's answer hinges on the relation of rhetoric to grammar and logic in various kinds of discourse, but the nature of that relation is characterized differently at different points of the *Anatomy*. Thus Frye's "perhaps" is rhetorically enacted rather than grammatically inscribed or logically deduced. The rhetorical enactment indeed begins with the very title identifying the book—a presumably non-literary work of criticism—as an example of one of the literary genres being discussed in it. Self-referentially enough, the *Anatomy* describes the "anatomy" as a specific form of prose fiction—a form that shares with Menippean satire the latter's generic "vision of the world in terms of a single intellectual pattern" (see 308-12, esp. 310).

In the compact introduction to the Fourth Essay, Frye outlines the intellectual pattern of his own vision of not just one world but three: the world of art is "flanked," he says, by the world of social action and events on one side, and by the world of individual thought and ideas on the other (243). A few additional triads, including Poe's Kantian Moral Sense/Taste/Pure Intellect, help to flesh out the basic trinitarian framework. Eventually Frye invokes "the traditional division of studies based on words into a 'trivium' of grammar, rhetoric, and logic" (244) — a division from which his attempt to define literature takes its conceptual departure.

In a bold, thought-provoking move, Frye extends the customary meaning of "grammar" and "logic" to cover the respective principles of sequential and conceptual order among words: grammar stands for the forward march of narrative; logic, for the retrospective mapping of the textual landscape just traversed. More in keeping with tradition, Frye distinguishes two kinds of rhetoric as the ornamental and the persuasive: "One articulates emotion; the other manipulates it." He finds that ornamental rhetoric is "inseparable" from literature because "most of the features characteristic of literary form, such as rhyme, alliteration, metre, antithetical balance, the use of exempla, are also rhetorical schemata." By contrast, persuasive rhetoric is "applied literature, or the use of literary art to reinforce the power of argument." Such use being generally "looked upon with some distrust," it is hardly surprising that "assertive, descriptive, or factual writing tends to be, or attempts to be, a direct union of grammar and logic." In light of the state of verbal affairs thus described, we are asked to "adopt the following tentative postulate: that if the direct union of grammar and logic is characteristic of non-literary verbal structures, literature may be described as the rhetorical organization of grammar and logic" (245).

So far so good. But when we reach the section called "The Rhetoric of Non-Literary Prose," our initial "tentative postulate" turns out to have been misguided. Rhetoric, and therefore literature, is now discovered to be inescapably involved with "anything which makes a functional use of words," that is to say, with all discourse (331). What Frye now argues is that a certain kind of "persuasive rhetoric" is rampant even in discourses that try hard to purify themselves of it. This kind of rhetoric (Frye calls it "conceptual") aims at the intellect rather than the emotions. Unlike the overtly "oratorical" rhetoric of, say, Johnson's letter to Chesterfield or Lincoln's Gettysburg address, "conceptual" rhetoric likes to disguise itself but can be detected in such devices of intellectual persuasion as the question-objection-answer scheme of Saint Thomas, or the orderly march of numbered propositions in Wittgenstein's *Tractatus*.

Some of Frye's additional examples for both the oratorical and the conceptual variety of persuasive rhetoric are far less dignified. On the overtly oratorical side, we encounter advertising, propaganda, and other attempts to sway our emotions toward a particular line of action; such attempts often rely on "hypnotic and incantatory" repetitions crass enough to resemble the speech rhythms of a boy training his dog (327). On the side of conceptual rhetoric, a bland "scholarly" prose style can be used to invoke the tough-minded authority of Reason Itself, while the likewise impersonal jargon of the bureaucrat's officialese pretends "to represent verbally the Institution or some anonymous cybernetic deity functioning in a state of 'normalcy.'" Since some ornamental or persuasive devices are present in all discourse directed to an audience, the Fourth Essay's last section — discussing what now appears to be misnamed "non-literary" prose — must come up with a new tentative postulate. It reads as follows: "If there is such a thing as conceptual rhetoric, which is likely to increase in proportion as the discursive writer tries to avoid it, it seems as though the direct union of grammar and logic, which we suggested at the beginning of this essay might be the characteristic of the non-literary verbal structure, does not, in the long run, exist. . . . The only road from grammar to logic, then, runs through the intermediate territory of rhetoric" (331).[1]

I find Frye's capacious concepts of grammar, logic, and rhetoric very helpful indeed. They enable us to reclaim the trivium from its most possessive abusers — grammar from the pedantic schoolteacher, logic from the formalistic philosopher, rhetoric from the political demagogue. In the enlarged sense of the three words grammar, logic, and rhetoric emerge as three intersecting dimensions of any well-formed, coherent, and effective discourse.[2] To be sure, etymology links grammar to writing, rhetoric to speech, and logic (through early Christian uses of *logos*) to thought as the mental presence of the unwritten and unspoken word.[3] Yet Frye's extension of the traditional meaning of the three terms suggests that each of the three principal guises of discourse—language written, thought, or spoken—is woven of all three kinds of thread: the threads of grammar, logic, and rhetoric. After all, whatever we "say"—be it in writing, speech, or silent deliberation—requires some degree of sequential order, conceptual coherence, and suasive power if it is to have a communicative impact on a particular audience.[4]

Frye's keen awareness of the intersubjective, rhetorical dimension of verbal practice makes him reject attempts to reduce grammar to logic or logic to grammar. Against the first type of reduction, he points out that reasoning is just "one of many things that man does with words, a specialized function of language." "There seems to be no evidence," he adds, "that man learned to speak primarily because he wanted to speak logically." Against the second type of reduction, Frye insists that, even though "logic may have grown out of grammar, . . . to grow out of something is in part to outgrow it." For example, the structure of English and other Indo-European languages forces us to speak and write about God and being (or about energy and matter) in grossly objectifying nouns. Yet we can expand our "logic" beyond the limits of our "grammar" by an effort to understand the more fluid linguistic conceptions of the Polynesian *mana* and the Iroquois *orenda* or the more precisely defined mathematical language of the physicist's equations concerning light and atoms (331-33).[5]

According to Frye, both grammar and logic develop through "internal conflict." We disentangle our ideas "from the swaddling clothes of their native syntax" by learning a foreign language and sharpen our conceptual vision through "dialectic, the principle of opposition in thought" (333).[6] Yet grammar and logic also have ties both to each other and especially to rhetoric. In a fancifully profound juxtaposition, Frye suggests that the initial link between grammar and rhetoric is "associative babble, in which sound and sense are equally involved," and that the corresponding link between logic and rhetoric is "doodle" or "associative diagram, the expression of the conceptual by the spatial" (334, 335).[7]

Babble on the one side, doodle on the other: the earful symmetry of this punning diagram is well prepared in the introduction to the Fourth Essay where Frye allies grammar with our listening to a quasi-temporal narrative sequence and logic with our envisioning a quasi-spatial conceptual pattern (244).[8] At the beginning of the section on "The Rhetoric of Non-Literary Prose," he further relates literature's internal *melos* and *opsis* (loosely translatable as poetic sound and poetic vision) to the "outer worlds" of *praxis* and *theoria*: the "appeal to action through the ear" and the "appeal to contemplation based predominantly on visual metaphors" (326, 327). Why not conclude (as I believe Frye almost does) that "babble" and "doodle" represent incipient efforts, which are not yet quite grammatical or quite logical, to establish rhetorical contact with a potential audience? As we engage in verbal babble or verbal doodle to bend someone's ear or to catch someone's mental eye, we occupy an essentially rhetorical "middle ground" between social action and individual thought. That middle ground of attempted communication is, then, something like a seed-plot out of which grammar and logic—formalized systems of verbal expression and conceptual articulation—keep emerging and continue to grow.[9]

On such a view, humans speak or write grammatically and logically in order to be in a better rhetorical position to "teach, delight, and move"—or whatever else they wish to accomplish by means of words.[10] This sounds plausible enough so long as we restrict our consideration to verbal interaction within a largely monolingual, socially and educationally homogeneous group. The members of each such group do indeed develop widely shared and fully internalized principles for the sequential and ideational organization of their communicative practice. Spontaneously applied, these principles need not be consciously recognized as grammatical and logical, and their rhetorical origin tends to be altogether obscured. But when certain ethnic, social, or educational outsiders attempt to communicate with the "in" group, their speech and writing will be perceived as ungrammatical and illogical unless they manage to suppress much of the "minority" grammar and logic peculiar to their own verbal dialect and conceptual dialectic (also known as world-view or ideology). Even privileged minorities face an analogous problem. For example, the grammar and logic employed in an expert grammarian's or logician's speech and writing may seem ingratiatingly flawless to the socially and educationally homogeneous group of admiring colleagues. Yet the same splendid grammar or logic could hinder more than help when employed to please or persuade members of some other group whose rhetorical impulse manifests itself in different grammatical or logical principles of ordering words in sequential and ideational patterns.

If my amplification of Frye's views in the preceding paragraph is valid, rhetoric will never dissolve into grammar and logic because no native speaker of a language can internalize all forms of grammar and logic—say, all dialects and ideologies—that other native speakers of the "same" language find particularly effective. Furthermore, bridging gaps between various linguistic and ideological subcultures of a single nation or civilization is only one function of rhetoric; it must also deal with some higher and many lower degrees of temporary incompatibility among potential communicators. Given two vastly different cultural horizons we cannot, as Frye wisely cautions, "walk into a Polynesian or Iroquois society and ask: 'What are *your* words for God, the soul, reality, knowledge?' They may have no such words or concepts, nor can we give them our equivalents for *mana* and *orenda*" (333). But Frye also notes that, even within the same culture, communication between any two persons will ultimately involve what he calls "the mental leap of metaphor away from the simple 'this means that' sign" (334). Communicative understanding does not occur by the reductive means of some "bilingual dictionary" in the mind (333). It requires, rather, the imaginative metaphorical identification of two meanings "of which each retains its own form" (334). All communication therefore entails metaphor—that Protean device of literary rhetoric which emerges from Frye's *Anatomy* as perhaps the most vital organ of any verbal intercourse.

It is clear that rhetorical appeals to emotion heavily rely on metaphor and other tropes. Yet Frye shows that even "conceptual rhetoric," that is, the supposedly nonrhetorical direct appeal of logical arguments to reason, cannot do without the metaphoric power of "doodle," or "associative diagram." Here is Frye's most extended example of the rhetorical "expression of the conceptual by the spatial": "If a writer says 'But on the other hand there is a further consideration to be brought forward in support of the opposing argument,' he may be writing normal (if wordy) English, but he is also doing precisely what the armchair strategist does when he scrawls plans of battle on a tablecloth" (335). The same strategy motivates, of course, familiar expressions like "let us now turn to" or "reverting to the point made earlier" (336): all such quasi-geometric phrases are designed to lead readers to apparently logical conclusions through the metaphorical space of conceptual rhetoric.

When Frye alerts us to the ploys of "conceptual rhetoric," he may be taken to suggest that rhetoric in fact separates grammar from logic—the sequential matter of the signifier from the conceptual pattern of the signified. But when he says that literature is "the rhetorical organization of grammar and logic," he clearly wants us to appreciate rhetoric as that which links grammar to logic in literary discourse and thereby links writers and readers to each other as simultaneous or successive participants in a literary tradition. The unifying power of literary rhetoric is further stressed when Frye portrays literature as "the use of language to express the completely integrated state of emotional consciousness we call imagination" (331). Let me spell out Frye's contrast between the literary and the nonliterary uses of rhetoric as follows: Whenever a speaker or writer is under the yoke of either unintegrated emotion or unintegrated intellect, or whenever a listener or reader is to be brought under such a yoke, nonliterary rhetoric splits person from person and fragments each person internally: it divides in order to rule us. But whenever literary rhetoric interconnects action and contemplation by splicing grammar with logic (the forward thrust of syntax with the backward glance of synopsis), the poles of emotion and intellect will have been brought close enough to one another for sparks of imaginative freedom to be generated within each speaker, writer, listener, and reader.[11]

"Whenever" is, of course, the wrong word to use in trying to make distinctions between the nonliterary and literary uses that we can make of rhetoric. After all, no discourse is likely to reach the extreme stage of being fully automatic or fully free, completely separating or totally integrating grammar and logic, emotion and intellect.[12] What I should have said is something like this: Rhetoric is nonliterary to the extent that it separates, and literary to the extent that it integrates, various aspects of "grammar" and "logic"—signifying sequence and signified pattern in the verbal signs, action-bent emotion and contemplative intellect in the human agents of signification. Such a premise could lead to at least three conclusions (each in keeping, I believe, with views expressed or implied by Frye himself): first, that all texts are somewhat literary and somewhat nonliterary; second, that the very same texts can be both produced and received with more or less literary attitudes; and third, that the question whether literature can be distinguished from nonliterature requires the tentative, open-ended answer "perhaps" rather than a definite, discussion-closing "yes" or "no."

Needless to say, many influential modern critics have said "yes" loud and clear—only to be forced to whisper subsequent allowances for blurred borderlines and mixed categories. In particular, I am thinking of the Russian Formalists, Czech Structuralists, and American New Critics, as well as some of their respective predecessors, fellow travelers, and disciples. These critics have attempted to define literariness on the respective bases of such promising concepts as defamiliarization, self-referentiality, or ambiguity, paradox, and irony. None of their proposed criteria could, however, be shown to apply to all (and nothing but) "literature." In part for this reason, quite a few recent critical votes have been cast against the possibility of rigorously distinguishing between literary and other kinds of discourse.[13] Since Frye's view of the matter seems to ally him with the latter camp, I will briefly contrast it to positions taken within that large and varied camp by Paul de Man and Terry Eagleton—two critics who, like Frye, approach the problem of literariness from the vantage point of their respective concepts of rhetoric.

Speaking of discourse in general, de Man repudiates the conventional wisdom that "grammar stands in the service of logic which, in turn, allows for the passage to the knowledge of the world." Such epistemological complacency is challenged, de Man says, as soon as "literariness, the use of language that foregrounds the rhetorical over the grammatical and the logical function, intervenes as a decisive but unsettling element" (*Resistance* 14). Generalized into the "figural potentiality" of all language, de Man's literariness pervades all communication as it "radically suspends logic and opens up vertiginous possibilities of referential aberration" (*Allegories* 10). On first hearing, these statements by Paul de Man could be taken to echo some of Frye's remarks quoted before. Yet Frye sees rhetorical figures as enabling (rather than subverting) a speaker's or writer's communicative interaction with a particular audience; he explicitly warns against "attempts to analyze metaphor solely to debunk an argument or suggest that it is 'nothing but' a metaphor" (*Anatomy* 337). Rather than obstructively "intervene" between grammar and logic, Frye's neighborly rhetoric serves as the "intermediate territory" through which many a "road from grammar to logic" may be built (*Anatomy* 331). For example, the quasi-temporal rhythms of oratorical rhetoric and the quasi-spatial patterns of conceptual rhetoric help us to erect efficient systems of grammar and logic, while our literary ways of integrating those rhythms and patterns through ornamental rhetoric eventually lead to systematic, even anatomizable, principles of poetic creativity.

Terry Eagleton's concept of rhetoric is very different from Paul de Man's. It does not make him see all discourse as literary; it makes him see all discourse—including literature— as political (see, for instance, *Literary Theory* 205). Far from being the theory and practice of referentially indeterminate troping, rhetoric for

Eagleton is "the theory of effective discourse and the practice of it." This rather traditional definition assumes new meaning because Eagleton's theoretical view of the practice of rhetoric is profoundly determined by his historical view of rhetorical theory as a pedagogical practice. It can certainly be argued that the teachable methods of rhetoric—the institutionalized "art of speaking and writing well in any discourse whatsoever"—emerged in ancient Greece and Rome for the purpose of the "textual training of the ruling class in the techniques of political hegemony" (*Walter Benjamin* 101-2). Even today, a good deal of what passes for verbal education appears to serve a similar purpose all over the world. Yet rhetoric and the study of rhetoric can clearly further emancipatory interests as well. As a radical socialist, Eagleton should, of course, be the last person to deny this. Unfortunately, however, he is so committed to disparaging what he calls, in the title of a recent essay, "the ideology of the aesthetic," that he seems especially hard put to appreciate the liberating potential of literary rhetoric both within and outside the realm of texts usually called literary. Thus much of what Frye values in verbal art as the prophetic projection of a "free, classless, and urbane" society (*Anatomy* 347) must strike Eagleton as the mystifying "imaginary resolution of real contradictions" (*Walter Benjamin* 107).[14]

Both the rhetoric of tropological indeterminacy and the rhetoric of political efficacy will prompt critics like de Man and Eagleton to deny any essential difference between what others may continue to call literary and nonliterary discourse. Now, Frye's concept of rhetoric, too, has much to do both with figurative language and situated communication. Why not add him to the nay-sayers on this thumbnail sketch of yea's and nay's variously expressed over the last several decades? It seems to me that even if the "grammar" of his diction and the "logic" of his imagery were more strongly suggesting the appropriateness of such classification, the "rhetoric" of his total argument would readily justify considering him as an implicit but articulate proponent of Perhaps. On the one hand, Frye does not hesitate to apply to literature the resolutely nonessentialist view that "it is convention, social acceptance, and the work of criticism in the broadest sense that determines" whether "a thing 'is' a work of art or not" (*Anatomy* 345). He also says that "all structures in words are partly rhetorical, and hence literary," so that "the notion of a scientific or philosophical verbal structure free of rhetorical elements is an illusion" (350). On the other hand, however, he does distinguish between the verbal automatism of disintegrative, nonliterary rhetoric and the integrative power of imaginative, literary rhetoric. That distinction may even seem to ally him with a particular group of yea-sayers: those New Critics who, following T. S. Eliot, nostalgically deplored "the dissociation of sensibility" which had supposedly occurred after the heyday of the English Metaphysical poets in the increasingly plebeian and secular seventeenth century.[15] It must be stressed, therefore, that Frye's vision of imaginatively integrated culture is utopian rather than nostalgic. In other words, his awareness of the always present danger of human fragmentation into mere emotion and sheer intellect is therapeutically forward-looking rather than causally tied to a consequential past affliction.

It is clear that Frye sees "babble" and "doodle"—unconnected emotion and intellect—as peripheral to the literary rhetoric of an integrated imagination. Yet his favored, literary center of discourse is not a fixed place at all—no "dead center" of the kind properly reserved by Dante for Lucifer, the "gentlemanly Prince of Darkness" (*Anatomy* 239). The expansive dynamism perceived by Frye as central to the verbal universe emerges, to adapt an image from Blake's *Marriage of Heaven and Hell*, as a kind of rhetorical Energy, for which grammatical and logical Reason serves as a temporary "bound or outward circumference" (149).[16] For Frye as for Blake, such bounding is always tentative and temporary because, as Blake put it, "Reason, or the ratio of all we have already known, is not the same that it shall be when we know more" (97).[17]

In the light of Blake's pertinent aphorisms—Frye comments on both in *Fearful Symmetry* (22, 46)—it would appear that the outward circumference of *ratio* must forever struggle to contain *oratio*—the continually growing field of discourses collectively expressive of what we know. In the *Anatomy*, however, Frye hints that a reverse state of containment has in fact been achieved. He concludes the section on "The Rhetoric of Non-Literary Prose" by suggesting that "nothing built out of words can transcend the nature and conditions of words" and that, therefore, "the nature and conditions of *ratio*, so far as *ratio* is verbal, are contained by *oratio*" (337).

When uttered or heard, the key words of the passage just cited rush to combine into playful paronomasia: *ratioratioratioratio* (and so forth). This piece of infinitely extendable "babble" seems ready, like the mystic's ouroboros, to go on and on swallowing its own tail.[18] Yet the pun's message is even more profoundly playful when it reaches us in the medium of the printed word. Facing the italicized doodle on the page, the reader actually sees that the longer word, *oratio*, contains the shorter *ratio*. In good cyclical fashion, *oratio* begins as both *oratio* and *ratio* end: with the appropriately circular letter *o*. And that hollow, graphically empty signifier does not function only as part of the alphabet. In the equally familiar symbol system of mathematics, whose ideogrammatic character Frye has just noted (333), the same cipher signifies "nothing," particularly when it precedes rather than follows other signifiers (zero-three, for instance, rather than three-zero pronounced thirty). Are we to understand that, in the end, *oratio* "contains" *ratio*, just as the circumference of *ratio* in turn bounds the energy of *oratio*, because there is, literally, zero difference between them? Perhaps, perhaps. Unless, of course, Yin and Yang, nonrhetorical literature and nonliterary rhetoric, differ to the extent that their dialectic escapes being swallowed up by some o-shaped, self-digestive serpent endlessly recycling in its rhetorical belly our logical space and grammatical time.

Notes

1 Frye's revocation of an initially postulated and presumably fundamental difference is analogous to a celebrated retraction in J. L. Austin's *How to Do Things with Words*. That study begins with the assumption that a clear distinction, in some ways not unlike Frye's distinction between literary and assertive writing, can be made between performative and constative speech acts. But in lecture 11 (133-147) Austin takes back most of what he appeared to give in lecture 1 (1-11). The structural parallel between the rhetorical strategies employed by the two authors is all the more remarkable because direct influence is quite unlikely: Austin's lectures were first delivered in 1955 and published posthumously in 1962; Frye's book was published in 1957.

2 It is tempting to see Frye's detrivialized trivium as the extension of three branches of linguistics: syntax, semantics, and pragmatics. In more precise semiotic terms, one might say that Frye's grammar and logic concern, respectively, the syntagmatic relations among signifiers and the paradigmatic relations among signifieds, while his rhetoric addresses the pragmatic relations between signs and sign users. Needless to add, the words *grammar*, *rhetoric*, and *logic* (however defined) can refer both to the subject matters of three disciplines and to the disciplines themselves, just as the word history can refer both to what happened and to an account or set of accounts of what happened.

3 "The Word (*logos*) was with God, and the Word was God" before it "was made flesh." John 1.1 and 1.14 can easily be seen as suggesting, among other things, the prelingual presence in the divine mind of whatever might later be spoken by the creator (e.g., "Let there be light") or written (both in the Bible and in the created world conceived as the "book of nature").

4 In the case of silent deliberation — Plato called it the dialogue of the soul with itself (see *Sophist* 263-64 and *Theaetetus* (189-90) — the audience is, of course, just one person. In "Doing, Making, Meaning: Toward a Theory of Verbal Practice," I enlist additional authorities in support of the dialogical dimension of quasi-verbal thinking.

5 In *Creation and Recreation*, Frye speculates that God should perhaps be conceived not as a noun, but as "a verb expressing a process fulfilling itself." He continues: "Such a use of language revives an archaic mode of language, and

yet is oddly contemporary with, for example, the language of the nuclear physicists, who no longer think of their atoms and electrons as things but as something more like traces of processes" (70).

6 See Ong, *Interfaces of the Word*: "Formal logic grew out of rhetoric and, more remotely, out of verbal combat, for formal logic came into being when the question was raised, Why is it that what you say demolishes what I say? What are the structures in play when yes and no are set in motion against one another?" (209).

7 Frye's concept of "doodle" as a halfway house between logic and rhetoric may have been influenced by historical observations like the following in Walter J. Ong's "Ramus and the Transit to the Modern Mind": "Ramus appears on the scene just when dialectic (logic) was shifting from an art of discourse ... to an art of thinking or reasoning. ... Dialectic was carried on in the privacy of one's own head and in a fashion more and more diagrammatic, with greater and greater reliance on spatial analogies and more or less overt desire to dispense with words as words, since these annoyingly hint that in some mysterious way thinking itself is always carried on in the presence—at least implicit—of another" (308-9). Strictly speaking, mental diagrams are relational rather than spatial because their actual size is indeterminate. Likewise, the temporal dimension of oral speech is reduced, both in writing and in thought, to a sequential order of unspecified duration. See also note 8 below.

8 "*Quasi*-temporal" and "*quasi*-spatial" are my terms, not Frye's. I use them to indicate that only the sequential order of words, not the speed of their delivery, is prescribed by Frye's "grammar" and that only the conceptual relation among meanings, not the scale of our mental map revealing that relation, is prescribed by Frye's "logic." Frye himself is less concerned with the unspecified duration of grammatical "time" and the indeterminate size of logical "space" than he is with those features of verbal discourse that clearly allow him to place literature between music and the visual arts. Even before defining grammar as "syntax or getting words in the right (narrative) order," and logic as "words arranged in a pattern with significance," he suggests two complementary renderings of the Greek word *lexis*: one pointing toward auditory *melos*, the other toward visual *opsis* (see Aristotle's *Poetics*, esp. ch. 6). *Lexis*, he says, "may be translated 'diction' when we are thinking of it as a narrative sequence of sounds caught by the ear, and as 'imagery' when we are thinking of it as forming a simultaneous pattern of meaning apprehended in an act of mental 'vision'" (244).

9 I take the image of seed-plot from Northrop Frye, who suggests in another context that life is the "seed-plot of literature, a vast mass of potential literary forms, only a few of which will grow up into the greater world of the literary universe" (122). Since he adds, "Similar universes exist for all the arts," it may be pertinent to suggest that not only arts like music and painting, but also arts like Frye's fully grown grammar and logic ("the art of ordering

words" and "the art of producing meaning," [244]) have their seeds planted in life—the rhetorical domain of human interaction. That is to say, the need or desire to communicate ("rhetoric") precedes the breaking up of what is to be said into the elements of an ordered verbal sequence ("grammar"), and the experience of hearing or reading a string of words in turn precedes our seeing the conceptual pattern of a text or utterance ("logic").

10 The individual words of the quoted phrase are repeatedly used in the *Defence of Poesie*, by Sir Philip Sidney, whose ultimate source for the poet's threefold purpose may well be Cicero's rhetorical triad of *probare, delectare, flectere*—the three "duties of the orator" that George Kennedy renders as prove, delight, and stir (100).

11 In Frye's spherical verbal universe, the literary freedom of integrated imaginative expression is diametrically opposed to the segregated "expression of reflex," which we approach whenever we depart from literature: "Whether we go in the emotional or in the intellectual direction, we arrive at much the same point, a point antipodal to literature in which language is a running commentary on the unconscious, like a squirrel's chatter" (331).

12 Frye says that "complete automatism" is the goal, presumably not quite achieved, of both "emotional jargon" and the "pseudo-logical simplification of language" caricatured in Orwell's *1984* as totalitarian "Newspeak" (331).

13 The eighteen essays I collected in *What Is Literature?* show the wide range of pertinent opinion prevailing in the 1970s; see also my "Literary Theory," esp. pp. 100-1 and 105-6).

14 Eagleton's unsympathetic treatment of Frye in *Literary Theory* (91-4) and elsewhere should be compared with another leading Marxist critic's much more favorable assessment; see Jameson, *The Political Unconscious*, 12, 68-75, et passim.

15 See Eliot, "The Metaphysical Poets": "in the seventeenth century a dissociation of sensibility set in, from which we have never recovered" (208).

16 "Energy is the only life, and is from the Body; and Reason is the bound or outward circumference of Energy" (*Marriage of Heaven and Hell*, Plate 4).

17 See "There Is No Natural Religion" (second series).

18 When I wrote this sentence, I did not realize that Frye himself had published a short piece on the ouroboros. For this reference, as well as several other bibliographical pointers, I am very grateful to Robert Denham. For further references to the ouroborous, see *Anatomy* 150, 157.

Works Cited

Austin, J. L. *How To Do Things with Words*. 2nd ed. Ed. J. O. Urmson and Marina Sbisa. Cambridge: Harvard UP, 1975.

Blake, William. *Complete Writings*. Ed. Geoffrey Keynes. 1966. Rev. paperback ed. London: Oxford UP, 1971.

de Man, Paul. *Allegories of Reading*. New Haven: Yale UP, 1979.

_____. *The Resistance to Theory*. Ed. Wlad Godzich. Minneapolis: U of Minnesota P, 1986.

Eagleton, Terry. "The Ideology of the Aesthetic." *Poetics Today* 9 (1988):

_____. *Literary Theory: An Introduction*. U of Minnesota P, 1983.

_____. *Walter Benjamin or Towards a Revolutionary Criticism*. London: NLB, 1981.

Eliot, T. S. *Selected Essays*. 3rd rev. ed. London: Faber, 1951.

Frye, Northrop. *Anatomy of Criticism: Four Essays*. Princeton: Princeton UP, 1957.

_____. *Creation and Recreation*. Toronto: U of Toronto P, 1980.

_____. *The Great Code: The Bible and Literature*. New York: Harcourt, 1982.

_____. "The Ouroboros." *Ethos* 1 (Summer 1983): 12-13.

Hernadi, Paul. "Doing, Making, Meaning: Toward a Theory of Verbal Practice." *PMLA* 103 (October 1988): 749-58.

_____. "Literary Theory." *Introduction to Scholarship in Modern Languages and Literatures*. Ed. Joseph Gibaldi. New York: MLA, 1981.

_____, ed. *What Is Literature?* Bloomington: Indiana UP, 1978.

Jameson, Fredric. *The Political Unconscious: Narrative as a Socially Symbolic Act*. Ithaca: Cornell UP, 1981.

Kennedy, George A. *Classical Rhetoric and Its Christian and Secular Tradition from Ancient to Modern Times*. Chapel Hill: U of North Carolina P, 1980.

Ong, Walter J. *Interfaces of the Word: Studies in the Evolution of Consciousness and Culture*. Ithaca: Cornell UP, 1977.

_____. "Ramus and the Transit to the Modern Mind." *The Modern Schoolman* 32 (May 1955).

Notes on Contributors

Hazard Adams is professor of English and comparative literature at the University of Washington, and cofounder and a senior fellow of the School of Criticism and Theory. Among his many books are *Philosophy of the Literary Symbolic* and *Joyce Cary's Trilogies*. He has edited *Critical Theory Since Plato* (1971) and *Critical Theory Since 1965* (1986).

Robert D. Denham is John P. Fishwick Professor of English at Roanoke College, where he edits the *Northrop Frye Newsletter*. He is the author of *Northrop Frye and Critical Method* and *Northrop Frye: An Annotated Bibliography of Primary and Secondary Sources* and the editor of three volumes of Northrop Frye's essays.

Paul Hernadi is professor of English and comparative literature at the University of California, Santa Barbara. He is the author of *Beyond Genre* and *Interpreting Events: Tragicomedies of History on the Modern Stage*, and has written a number of essays examining Frye's taxonomies of literary conventions.

Patricia Parker is professor of English at Stanford University. She is the author of *Inescapable Romance: Studies in the Poetics of a Mode* and *Literary Fat Ladies: Rhetoric, Gender, Property*, and has coedited volumes of essays on lyric poetry and poststructuralist criticism, Shakespeare and theory, and Renaissance texts and critical theory. Professor Parker also contributed to the *Festschrift* for Frye, *Centre and Labyrinth*.

Imre Salusinszky is lecturer in English at the University of Newcastle, Australia. His publications include a book of interviews, *Criti-*

cism in Society. He is currently preparing a book on Frye for Routledge's "Critics in the Twentieth Century" series.

David Staines is professor of English at the University of Ottawa. He is the author of *Tennyson's Camelot: The "Idylls of the King" and Its Medieval Sources*, has written numerous articles on medieval literary topics, and has edited two volumes of essays on Canadian literature, *The Canadian Imagination* and *The Forty-Ninth and Other Parallels.*

Hayden White is professor in the department of History of Consciousness at the University of California, Santa Cruz. He is the author of *Metahistory* and *Tropics of Discourse*, and his numerous essays on philosophy of history frequently draw on Frye's theories of emplotment and modes.

Thomas Willard is associate professor of English at the University of Arizona. A former student of Northrop Frye, he was a contributor to the volume *Centre and Labyrinth: Essays in Honour of Northrop Frye*, and has edited the works of Jean D'Espagnet.

Index